D1483577

Mary, Queen of Scots

Mary
Queen of Scots

Gordon Donaldson

with a foreword by
A. L. Rowse

 The English Universities Press Ltd

ISBN 0 340 12383 4

First published 1974

The English Universities Press Ltd
St Paul's House, Warwick Lane, London EC4P 4AH
Printed in Great Britain by Hazell Watson & Viney Ltd
Aylesbury, Bucks

Foreword

Mary Queen of Scots has been far too much written about by non-historians. Her romantic personality and tragic career have had a great appeal for poets, dramatists and general biographers; but it is time that the subject should be dealt with by a professional historian, particularly a Scottish historian.

For it was Scotland that was the scene of her active career as a ruler, from 1561 to 1567. The years before in France were really a prologue to the drama in Scotland, while the twenty years' confinement in England were but a long epilogue. And these, once she had lost power, were of much less real importance than they are usually given in books about her. In politics power is what is important, and Mary lost much of her importance when she lost her throne.

Yet her career has usually been treated from the English perspective.

Not so with this book. Its special value is that it deals with her from the point of view of the country of which she was the ruling Queen – like her senior and cousin, Elizabeth in England, with whom Mary Stewart's career was fatally entangled. Mary had a more difficult task in Scotland, where the Crown had much less authority and far smaller resources; and she made a fair success of it until her disastrous marriage to Darnley engendered her downfall. All the same, she produced the heir, James VI and I, with whom the union of the two kingdoms was ultimately accomplished. So her life, in spite of its adventures and disasters, was not without fruit: her place in history is assured.

With this book we have it presented, with both sympathy and justice, by the leading Scottish historian today. It is written from

27092

the perspective of the affairs of his country, without confessional bias. We see a small indication of his point of view in his insistence on the spelling Stewart, where the English use the form Stuart: Professor Donaldson's usage draws attention to the origin of the name, as 'stewards' to the ancient Royal house of Scotland.

Mary has been the victim of partisanship on both sides, Presbyterian and Catholic, English and Scottish, in her posthumous career at the hands of historians as in her lifetime. At last we have a biography which rises above partisanship to do her historic justice.

A. L. ROWSE

Contents

Plates

Acknowledgments

The author and publisher wish to thank the following for permission to reproduce the illustrations in this book : The Depart-
ment of the Environment, Edinburgh, plates I, XII, XIII (Crown
copyright reserved); Roger-Viollet, Paris, plates II, V; Bibliotheque
Nationale, Paris, plates III, IV; J. Allan Cash, plate VI; the Scottish
National Portrait Gallery, plates VIII, XIV; the Public Record
Office, plate XI (Crown copyright reserved). Plate VII is reproduced by gracious permission of H.M. Queen. Plates IX, X are
from a private collection and are reproduced by permission of
the owner.

1 Prelude: The Reign of James V

Mary Stewart was a sovereign who hardly ever exercised sovereignty. The first eighteen years of her life were shaped by the pattern of international relations, when France and England each sought, sometimes by war and sometimes by diplomacy, to make Scotland a satellite, and the end of this phase found Mary the consort of the French king. After her first husband's death in December 1560 she returned to Scotland to rule as Queen until her surrender at Carberry in June 1567. Then, for almost the last twenty years of her life, she was a prisoner whose own actions could of themselves do little to influence the course of events. Thus, in a lifetime of just over forty-four years, Mary had a measure of freedom of action for less than seven, and even when she ruled in person in Scotland her ability to shape policy was circumscribed by the people and institutions of the country. To say that Mary's life was largely determined by events over which she had no control is not the same as saying that she was the victim of circumstances, for her biography is the study of the interplay between her, as woman and queen, and the national and international situations. But she must never be thought of as the maker of her own destiny, for her fortunes were shaped at least as much by events as by any qualities or defects in her character, or by anything she did or left undone.

The conditions in which Mary was to live and reign and die had been to a great extent determined before she was born, during the lifetime of her father, James V. For the Scots it was a period of decision: should they cast off the Papacy, break their ancient alliance with France, embrace the Reformation, and come to terms with England? For more than two centuries

Scotland's history had been very largely shaped by her relations with England and France. England was the 'old enemy', whose repeated attempts to conquer Scotland had inflicted on the Scots many heavy defeats but were in the end successfully resisted. France, if only because she also was England's enemy and, like Scotland, a target for English attempts at conquest, was Scotland's 'old ally', tied to Scotland by a treaty made so early as 1295 and many times renewed. The Franco–Scottish alliance committed the two countries to mutual assistance against English aggression, and in practice many Scots gave military service in France, while French forces occasionally came to Scotland.

After two hundred years of Anglo-Scottish warfare, the six-teenth century had opened with the promise of better things, in a treaty of perpetual peace and the marriage of James IV to Margaret Tudor, elder daughter of Henry VII. The ultimate result of the marriage was the accession of the great-grandson of James and Margaret, James VI, to the throne of England in 1603; but the immediate outcome was less happy, for only ten years after the treaty of perpetual peace with England the Scots again invaded that country in terms of their treaty with France. While the Franco–Scottish treaty looked equitable on paper, the French had tended on the whole to invoke it only when it suited them to stimulate the Scots into making attacks on England which would divert English attention from the Con-tinent. On this, the last occasion when the Scots were thus prevailed on to serve as a French tool, they were heavily de-feated and their king, James IV, killed at Flodden. James V succeeded to the Scottish throne at the age of seventeen months. His mother was heiress to the English crown, failing issue of her brother, Henry VIII, and the heir presumptive to England was to be found in the Scottish royal line during most of the rest of the century, indeed all of it except the twenty-five years be-tween the birth of Elizabeth Tudor in 1533 and the death of her sister Mary in 1558. The prospects of the Stewart dynasty were never far from men's minds, and on the whole there was a stronger case for Anglo-Scottish amity when the English succession seemed likely to fall to Scots: Scotland tended to be less compliant with England when this contingency was more remote.

James V's fifteen-year minority was a singularly troubled one, in which the rivalries of factions among the Scottish nobility interacted with French and English policies. After Flodden some Scots began to reflect that the old alliance had been a one-sided affair, and never again could the Scottish nobles be stirred to enthusiasm for crossing that fatal frontier and risking a repetition of the disaster of 1513. This was one reason for the emergence in Scotland of a party which thought that the orientation of Scotland's foreign policy should be reconsidered. Yet some years passed before we can speak with confidence of a 'French party' and an 'English party', for it was rare for an individual or group to adhere with anything like consistency to one or the other, and political principles or convictions were seldom paramount. The French cause was represented by the King's cousin John, Duke of Albany, 'the Scot who was a Frenchman', who had been born in France and came to Scotland after Flodden to be governor of the realm. Henry VIII rightly saw in Albany the chief obstacle to his schemes for controlling Scotland, but the duke was much hampered by the vicissitudes of Anglo-French relations, since France would allow him freedom of action in Scotland only when she was at war with England, and from 1517 to 1521 he was actually detained in France at Henry's behest.

The Queen Mother, Margaret Tudor, seemed obviously cast for the part of an agent for her brother Henry VIII, and she did often act in the English interest, but she was far too capricious to be credited with political motives, far less statesmanship, and she took as her second husband Archibald, sixth Earl of Angus, who was characterized as 'a young witless fool'. For the brief period when the relations between Margaret and Angus were harmonious they together represented the English cause, but they soon drifted apart and thereafter were invariably to be found in opposite camps. Margaret, although she participated in a pro-English administration in 1524, had previously been in political association with the pro-French Albany. Angus for his part sometimes supported France, but he ultimately headed a pro-English administration which ruled Scotland in the last years of the minority and held the King a captive. In 1517 Albany had concluded the Treaty of Rouen, whereby the prospects of marriage to a daughter of the French king were held out to James V, but he found that the Scots, recalling how the French alliance had in 1513 led them into a war they had not sought, had lost their taste for adventures across the Border and twice declined to follow him when he proposed to invade England on behalf of France. On the whole the indications are that pro-English feeling was growing, and, while England's friends were often merely serving their personal ends, the publication in 1521 of John Major's *Greater Britain* represented serious propaganda in favour of amity between England and Scotland and their union through a dynastic link.

The growth of the pro-English faction was soon encouraged by the onset of the Reformation. Already in the 1520s the teachings of Luther were reaching Scotland, and within a decade many prominent Scots were committed to the reforming cause. After Henry VIII had repudiated papal supremacy, those Scots who favoured the Reformation saw in England an example, and some of them, at odds with the authorities in their own country, found in England a refuge. On the other hand, those whose ecclesiastical opinions were conservative tended to favour the old alliance with France.

More generally, the whole of Scottish policy during James V's personal rule was affected by relations with foreign powers and with a Reformation which had become an international movement, and both international relations and the ecclesiastical situation gave James peculiarly favourable opportunities. At this time the pattern of alliance and hostility among the European powers was particularly unstable. The old alliance of Scotland with France had been maintained when Anglo-French hostility had been a constant factor, but in the sixteenth century the threat to France came no longer from England but from the house of Hapsburg, which ruled not only the Imperial dominions but also Spain and the Low Countries. Thus France and the Emperor sought English support, and, while England played off one against the other, the power which was for the time being hostile to England was apt to make a bid for a Scottish alliance, and France, in the periods when she was anxious to appease England, was ready to sacrifice the interests of her old allies the Scots.

The Reformation introduced a fresh complication. Henry VIII's breach with Rome for a time made it difficult for him to come to terms with the Emperor Charles V, who was the nephew of Henry's discarded wife, Catherine of Aragon, and the Pope began to press for an alliance of France and the Empire in a crusade against schismatic England. Besides, when the Pope saw England, as well as parts of Germany and Scandinavia, slipping from his grasp, he was ready to go to any lengths to retain the loyalty of other countries, including Scotland. Henry VIII, for his part, wanted to win James of Scotland to support his anti-papal policy.

In these circumstances, Scotland had a temporary importance out of all proportion to its wealth or strength, and James exploited the situation with considerable skill. It seems very likely that his own preference was for a French alliance and for orthodoxy. French Albany had appointed James's tutor, Gavin Dunbar, who in 1524, on Albany's recommendation, became archbishop of Glasgow, and it was this prelate, who must have represented a pro-French influence, whom James selected as his chancellor in 1528. Albany himself was not in Scotland after 1524, when James was twelve, but he continued to act as a Scottish agent and he was connected by marriage with the Medici family, to which Pope Clement VII (1523–1534) belonged. In any event, James may well have had happier recollections of Albany's régime in Scotland than he had of that of Angus, his stepfather, whose pro-English administration had kept him captive for two years. James's antipathy to Angus, who found a refuge in England after his fall in 1528, as well as against Angus's kinsmen in Scotland, was unrelenting, and this must have predisposed him against England. One final fact which must have inclined the King to the French side was the existence of the Treaty of Rouen, under which he could expect the brilliant prize of the French king's daughter as a bride.

So far as religion was concerned, James combined a licentious life with conventional observances and devotions, and it is hard to believe that Protestant teaching would have any attractions for him. He was not unaware of the moral shortcomings of the Scottish clergy and of the unrest caused by the financial exactions of a corrupt Church, to the extent that at one stage he is said to have rounded on the prelates: 'Wherefore gave my predecessors so many lands and rents to the kirk? Was it to maintain hawks, dogs, and whores to a number of idle priests?' Yet, far from countenancing the preachers of reform, he consented to a number of prosecutions of heretics and to a few executions. However, while James's preference was thus for the French alliance and for orthodoxy, he was, perhaps above all, anxious to replenish his coffers after the utterly ruinous financial administration of the minority and he exacted his price for his adherence to those causes.

The price of orthodoxy was a share in the wealth of the Church. There was certainly a direct connection between Henry VIII's recognition by the Convocation of Canterbury, in February 1531, as 'Supreme Head of the Church of England so far as the law of Christ allows' and the decision of the Pope, within a matter of months, to permit James to exact levies from the Church on an unprecedented scale. Nevertheless, the Pope's generosity had an additional motive. Albany had had a plan to marry James to his niece, Catherine de' Medici, the ward of the Pope, and she could be expected to bring a large dowry. However, the Pope had no enthusiasm for letting Catherine depart for a distant and chilly country, while the French king knew that his own hold over James would be loosened if he could no longer sway him by the prospect of a French marriage, and he therefore negotiated for the marriage of Catherine to his own son, afterwards Henry II.

The Pope, knowing well enough that the interest of the Scots was less in Catherine's person than in her dowry, decided to

offer them financial compensation, and that without dipping
into his own pocket. The upshot was that James received first
a grant of a tenth of the revenues of all ecclesiastical benefices
in Scotland for three years, ostensibly for the defence of the
realm, and then an annual payment of £10,000 from the
bishoprics and abbeys, ostensibly for the endowment of the
Court of Session, the central civil court, as a 'College of Justice'.
The proposed annual levy of £10,000 was in practice compounded for by a lump sum of £72,000 and a small annual payment in perpetuity. The King on his side undertook to defend
'the sete of Rome and halikirk' and the Scottish parliament,
remarking with truth that, whereas earlier popes had been
generous in their days, Pope Clement was more gracious and
benevolent than all his predecessors, dutifully recorded the
King's undertaking. In 1532 the Pope conceded that no Scottish
cases were to be called to Rome in the first instance, but were to
be heard by ecclesiastics appointed by the King. Even these
concessions were not the limit of papal generosity. Still in 1532,
when James was barely twenty, he wrote to the Pope, remarking
on the frailty of human nature and intimating that he had three
small sons for whose welfare he was much concerned, and he
requested a dispensation for their promotion to any ecclesiastical benefices; the only qualification was that they were not
to become bishops or archbishops under the age of twenty. As
the years passed, and the King's family increased, no less than
six of his progeny were provided for in this way, so that the
revenues of several of the richest religious houses in Scotland
were in effect augmenting the royal exchequer. In 1535 the
Pope formally conceded the King's right to nominate to all
bishoprics and abbeys, and this meant a conspicuous increase
in the royal patronage which was such a valuable instrument in
the management of Scotland.

The price of adherence to France was the desired French marriage. James pursued many matrimonial schemes, and even considered marrying one of his mistresses, but only a continental
marriage could yield the necessary dowry, and the likelihood is
that all the alternatives to a French marriage, while not frivo-

lous, were mainly of value as levers to induce Francis to concede his daughter Madeleine. More than one of the proposed
matches was with a kinswoman of the Emperor, and this would
be unwelcome to France and England alike. Another proposal,
for a marriage to Mary, daughter of Henry VIII, was a direct
incentive to France to make a counter-offer. Henry was not
likely to throw away the great prize of his daughter and heiress
on James, but he tried very hard to accommodate him in other
ways. The proposed marriage to Catherine de' Medici was a
compromise concocted by Albany, who did not want to see
his cousin making either an Imperial or an English match, but
knew that at the time a French marriage was impossible. France
wanted to prevent an Imperial alliance, but when she was
friendly with England she could not afford to arrange a French
marriage for James. Besides, Francis was genuinely reluctant to
part with the fragile Madeleine, and kept putting James off
without actually closing the door. Just how James was raising
his price and being courted by foreign sovereigns is illustrated
by the fact that he received the Order of the Golden Fleece from
the Emperor, the Order of the Garter from Henry, and the
Order of St Michael from Francis.

In 1535 the Anglo-French alliance broke down and France
and the Emperor were at war. This made France ready to look
afresh at her relations with Scotland, and terms were reached
for a marriage of James to Mary, the daughter of the Duke of
Vendome, with a very large dowry to compensate for her lack
of good looks. James set out for France in 1536 to claim his
bride, but the marriage which took place was not to Mary, whom
James found *bossue et contrefaicte* (hunchbacked and mis-
shapen). His personal appeals may have moved Francis and the
attractions of this lively young king certainly captivated Madeleine, whose happiness her father could not bring himself to
ignore. So the marriage to Madeleine took place on 1 January
1537. She arrived in Scotland with James in May, but died after
six weeks. There seems to have been no hesitation in pursuing
a second French marriage, and the negotiations were carried
through by David Beaton, nephew and coadjutor of the Arch-

bishop of St Andrews and a leader of pro-French and orthodox opinion. The second French bride was Mary, daughter of Claude, Duke of Guise. She had recently been widowed by the death of her first husband, the Duke of Longueville, and a match had been proposed between her and Henry VIII, who had recently lost his third wife, Jane Seymour. Mary of Guise – 'of the largest stature of women' – had a tall and well-proportioned figure. When Henry suggested that a marriage to him would be ap-priate since he was a well-built man and should have a well-built wife, Mary is said to have retorted, 'Yes, but my neck is small.'

James had acquired a French bride; he had acquired two dowries. This was the price for his committing his country to the cause of France and the Papacy, and a few days after the marriage to Madeleine the Pope sent him a sword and a cap, with an intimation that he expected Scottish participation in a campaign against Henry VIII. In 1538, when France and the Emperor made peace, it seemed possible that they might make an alliance for a crusade against England, and the time was thought ripe for the Pope to excommunicate the English King.

Henry, confronted with the possibility of large-scale attack from the Continent, was more anxious than ever to avoid en-circlement and to detach Scotland from continental allies. He had already been endeavouring to induce James to follow his example in ecclesiastical policy, and when he dissolved the monasteries he was at some pains to point out to his nephew the advantages to be derived from such action. But James had less to gain than Henry calculated, for owing to papal benevo-lence so much of the Church's wealth was already at his dis-posal that there was no need for a breach with Rome. However, some Scots, for both political and religious reasons, did favour imitation of England, and they persuaded James to agree to meet Henry at York. The council, who feared kidnapping, refused to let James leave the country, and the Scottish churchmen put for-ward their arguments, reinforcing them by lavish promises of financial support for war against England. James therefore did not go to York. Henry, who made the long journey north and had made it in vain, was understandably furious, and war was the result.

Meantime, the continental coalition against England had dissolved. David Beaton was sent to France for help, but came back empty-handed, and Scotland had to face England without allies. Not only so, but the Scotland which James attempted to lead to battle was divided. There had now taken shape two distinct parties – a conservative or Roman Catholic party, looking to France and willing to see Scotland used against Henry VIII, and a reforming party, which thought that Scotland should follow English example in ecclesiastial affairs and should stand with England against the papalist powers of the Continent. The divided state of Scotland goes a long way to explain the disastrous end of James V's reign. But it is not the whole explanation. Too many Scots distrusted their King. James had followed a policy of severity and acquisitiveness which was highly impolitic in a country where the central administration was weak and government could be carried on successfully only by conciliation. All men of position and substance feared, and had no reason to love, James V, 'so sore a dread King and so ill-beloved of his subjects'. James lives in memory as 'the poor man's king', but the poor men of Scotland could have done little to save him from powerful enemies; the nobility, besides being antagonized by his harshness, were alienated by the preference he showed for administrators of middle-class origin; and there were many men of all ranks – among them three hundred and fifty nobles and barons whose names appeared, so it was said, in a 'black list' – who were tainted with heresy and were apprehensive about this orthodox and acquisitive monarch.

When the war opened, James could not carry his subjects with him. Faced by the reluctance of the nobles to invade England, he had to rely largely on an army financed by the churchmen and commanded by his latest favourite, Oliver Sinclair. The army crossed the Border, to be routed on 24 November 1542 at Solway Moss, in an encounter where some Scots seem actually to have preferred to surrender rather than fight in an unpopular cause for a king in whom they had no confidence.

Although James was described by some writers of his own day as strong and courageous in body and spirit, the disaster and disgrace of Solway Moss brought him rapidly to complete collapse. He retired from the Borders to Edinburgh, to Linlithgow (where he spent a week with his queen), and at last to Falkland. He had no will to live, and declined to make any arrangements for Christmas, because, as he said, by that time the realm would be masterless. It brought him no cheer that on 8 December Mary of Guise gave birth to a daughter at Linlithgow.

James had lost his first wife, and the two sons borne to him by his second wife had died within a few days of each other in 1541. He had six illegitimate sons and two daughters alive at the time of his death, and one illegitimate son seems to have predeceased him. The record of his bastard brood suggests that they may have derived from their father some physical weakness which they shared with their half-sister Mary. One son, James, Commendator of Kelso and Melrose, died when he was about twenty-six, and John, Commendator of Coldingham, died when he was thirty or thirty-one. James, Commendator of St Andrews, was cut off by an assassin when he was apparently still in his full vigour at thirty-eight. Adam, Commendator of the Charterhouse, lived to be about forty, and Robert, Commendator of Whithorn, lived until he was over forty, but from the small part they played in affairs it seems a reasonable inference that both of them, especially Robert, suffered from some infirmity, either physical or mental. The only son to reach what would then have been regarded as old age was Robert, Commendator of Holyrood, who did not die until 1593, when he must have been nearly sixty.

If most of James V's family thus died early, as their father had done, it is also true that they produced few offspring. James of St Andrews had three daughters, only one of whom had issue; John (whose marriage lasted less than two years) had apparently only one lawful son; James of Kelso and Melrose had no children, and the same appears to be true of Adam and of Robert of Whithorn. The only one to be at all prolific was

Robert of Holyrood, who counterbalanced his brothers by having no less than nineteen children, but even in this case the next generation showed signs of petering out, for Robert's eldest son died in his father's lifetime and his second son had no legitimate issue. It is difficult to escape the conclusion that Mary, Queen of Scots, was born into a family with some inherent weakness which seemed to mark it out for extinction.

But James V, as he lay dying at Falkland on 14 December 1542, could see only his dead boys, his newborn daughter, and his growing bastards. The failure of legitimate male issue and the prospective end of the Stewart dynasty, in contrast to the survival of his illegitimate brood, may have been one of the reflections which darkened and embittered his last hours. Some contemporary reports have it that he reviewed in his mind the errors of his policy in exiling Angus, forfeiting nobles and imprisoning men who might have served him well. But, according to the more picturesque narrators, his regrets were personal rather than political, and centred on the disgrace of his favourite, Oliver Sinclair, at Solway, and on the birth of his daughter. They tell how he moaned, 'Fy, fled Oliver? Is Oliver tane? All is lost'; how he received the news of his daughter's birth with the words, 'It came with a lass, it will pass with a lass'; and how he turned his back to his lords and his face to the wall. He died on 14 December 1542, 'a worn-out, desperate man, at the age of thirty years'.

The Minority: Scotland,
       England and France

In James V's last days the pro-French and papalist party had been
in control under the leadership of Cardinal Beaton, and, although
discredited by the disaster at Solway, it made an attempt to
maintain its ascendancy by claiming that James, on his death-
bed, had committed the regency to the cardinal and his nominees.
Mystery surrounds the affair, but, while Beaton may not have
gone so far as to cause 'a dead man's hand to subscribe a blank' –
that is, to sign a commission with a space in which the names of
regents could be inserted – there does exist a notarial instrument,
dated on the day of James's death, which relates that the King
named as the cardinal's colleagues in the government the Earl
of Moray (James's half-brother), the Earl of Huntly, and the Earl
of Argyll. This pointedly excluded James Hamilton, Earl of
Arran, although, as the eldest descendant of James II's daughter
Mary, he had been heir presumptive since the death of the Duke
of Albany in 1536 and had therefore almost a prescriptive right
to be Governor of the Realm in the minority. Arran was in the
cardinal's black books, for his name had evidently headed a list
of heretics which Beaton had handed to the late King. A fortnight after James's death Arran was reported to have drawn
his sword on Beaton and charged him with being 'a false churl'
who told many lies 'in the King's name'; and the Hamiltons
certainly repudiated as invalid the notarial instrument appoint-
ing regents, for it is endorsed 'Sir Henry Balfour instrument that
was never notar'.

The attempted *coup* by the conservative party proved abor-
tive, not because of opposition from Arran or anyone else in
Scotland, but because of the return from England not only of

the lords who had surrendered to the English at Solway but also
of the Earl of Angus, who had been an exile since the fall of his
administration in 1528. Henry VIII had lost no time in sending
for Angus and grooming him for a resumption of his old role
as leader of a pro-English party in Scotland, and the Solway
captives were released on condition that they would support
the marriage of Mary to Prince Edward, Henry's five-year-old
son and heir. At least some of them went further and undertook
to help Henry to secure Scotland for himself or for Edward in
the event of Mary's death. These pro-English magnates were
received by Arran on 25 January, and a day or two later the
cardinal (who had become Chancellor on 10 January) was deprived of power and arrested. In March a parliament met which
declared Arran Second Person in the Realm and Governor until
the Queen's 'perfect age', which was understood to mean the
completion of her twelfth year. Arran had already come into
the open with support for church reform: he declared that for
five years he had considered the Pope to be nothing more than
'a very evil bishop', and he authorized a friar to preach in favour
of the vernacular Bible. Parliament, stimulated by advice from
England to 'let slip among the people' the Bible in English, permitted the lieges to read the Scriptures in 'English or Scots', and
this was taken as a signal for attacks on religious houses. Sir
Ralph Sadler, Henry's envoy, who arrived in Edinburgh as an
advocate of his master's wishes, received Holy Communion in
company with Arran, and commissioners were appointed to
begin negotiations for the marriage of Mary to Edward.

But the triumph of the English and reforming party had
precarious foundations. Sadler had not been two days in Edinburgh when he reported that high-handed action would put all
to hazard, for if the Scots were threatened with subjection to
England 'there is not so little a boy but he will hurl stones against
it, and the wives will handle their distaffs and the commons
universally will rather die.' While many Scots might be sufficiently pro-English to approve in principle their Queen's marriage to the English heir, with its prospects of peace instead of
recurrent war, they wanted to preserve their country's identity

and they saw no reason why Mary should not be brought up in her native land. The negotiations took the line that Scotland was not to be absorbed into England, but was to have its own parliament, courts, laws, and liberties and that, should there be no children of the marriage, Mary's heirs were to succeed in Scotland. But Henry handled a delicate situation with singular ineptitude, and showed an anxiety to assume the custody of Mary's person which looked suspicious. He wanted her to cross the Border almost as soon as she could leave the care of her mother, but the Scots, who knew that if she passed into English custody prematurely all the safeguards for the integrity of Scotland might be nullified, wanted her to remain in Scotland until she could 'complete marriage'. By the Treaties of Greenwich, concluded on 1 July, it was arranged that she should leave for England when she reached the age of ten.

Apart from resentment and suspicion, opposition to the proEnglish policy came from a number of notables besides the temporarily captive cardinal. They disapproved of the rehabilitation of the Angus Douglases and of the imprisonment of Beaton, and they stayed away from the March parliament. The Queen Mother, too, whose maternal rights towards her infant daughter could not be ignored, was using her influence in favour of the French alliance and sowing mistrust between Arran and Henry. By the end of March Beaton was back in his own castle of St Andrews, under no more than a nominal restraint, and he was soon at large and able to lead the clergy into making an offer of financial assistance for defence against England. Before the end of July, in association with the lords opposed to the Governor, he was able to engineer the removal of the Queen and her mother from Linlithgow to Stirling, where there was greater security against any sudden raid by the English.

But even if the conservative party could have the custody of the Queen's person, Scottish policy could be changed only by prevailing on Arran, the lawful governor, to break off the negotiations with England. It is unlikely that he had strong convictions about either the Reformation or the English alliance, and on reflection he may very well have had some doubts in his own mind about the policy which the pro-English party had persuaded him to adopt. He certainly could not sacrifice his prospects of the reversion of the crown by accepting any agreement which would assign the Scottish succession, failing issue of Mary and Edward, to Edward's heirs; and besides, if Mary meantime remained in Scotland, much might happen in the twelve years or so before she reached marriageable age, while, if the English negotiations broke down, she might be married to Arran's own son and heir, the Master of Hamilton, a boy about the same age as Edward.

Apart from any such calculation of his own, Arran was peculiarly vulnerable to pressure because of one weakness in his position: he was the son of his father's third marriage and, as there was some dubiety about the validity of the elder Arran's divorce from his second wife, the Governor's legitimacy could be called in question. The return from France of Matthew Stewart, fourth Earl of Lennox, who stood next to Arran in the line of succession, may have been intended to serve as an object lesson: he certainly was brought over deliberately by the pro-French party, in secrecy and with supplies from France. Besides, Arran's half-brother, John, Commendator of Paisley, who also came back from France, was a far more intelligent man than the Governor and seems to have been persuaded by Beaton that the dynastic interests of the family would be best served by adhering to France and the Pope. It could hardly be doubted that the best defence against the threat from Lennox lay in an accommodation with the cardinal, who, as a papal legate and as head of the Scottish ecclesiastical system, could pronounce on matters of matrimony and legitimacy. The irresolute Arran was soon wavering: 'What the English lords decide him to do one day, the abbot [John Hamilton] changes the next.'

Henry VIII was not idle, and tried to counteract French pressure by offers of his own: the Master of Hamilton might marry the Princess Elizabeth; Arran could have 5,000 English troops to put down opposition to the English marriage proposals; and, if Henry had to resort to force and conquer Scotland, Arran could be king beyond the Forth. Arran had his doubts, for he thought that £5,000 would be more useful than 5,000 men, and a largely Highland kingdom had limited attractions for a Low-lander. He was at last induced, on 25 August, to ratify the treaties, but it was characteristic of his inconstancy that little more than a week later – in the words of an indignant Pro-testant –

the unhappy man . . . quietly stole away from the lords that were with him in the palace of Holyroodhouse, passed to Stirling, sub-jected himself to the Cardinal and his counsel, received absolution, renounced the profession of Christ Jesus his holy Evangel and violated his oath that before he had made for observation of the contract and league with England.

The renewed concord between Church and State provided a suitable atmosphere for the coronation of the young Queen at Stirling on 9 September 1543 – the thirtieth anniversary of the battle of Flodden.

It remained for the Scottish parliament to accept the *volte-face*. Henry, by his hectoring and high-handed attitude, had given the Scots ample grounds for resiling from the agreement. They objected to his demand that they should formally break the traditional alliance with France; his offer to Arran of 5,000 English soldiers would, it was said, cause 20,000 Scots to come out on the other side; Scottish ships which had put to sea trust-ing that the peace was effective were seized by the English government; and England failed to ratify the agreement of 1 July within the prescribed period of two months. On 11 Decem-ber the Scottish parliament, on the grounds of the seizure of the ships and the delay in ratifying the agreement, denounced the alliance with England and reaffirmed that with France. The Master of Hamilton had been placed in the cardinal's castle of St Andrews as a kind of hostage for his father's good behaviour, and Arran was to be advised by a council, containing Beaton (who was reappointed as Chancellor) and Mary of Guise. The Governor had already been taken by the cardinal to Dundee to deal with attacks on friaries, and an Act was now passed urging proceedings against heretics and affirming Arran's readiness to do his part. This was in December, and a francophile policy may have received some stimulus from an event which happened in France in January. Catherine de' Medici, wife of the King of France, after ten years of barren wedlock, gave birth to a son. Here was an obvious rival to Edward of England.

But the Scots were far too deeply divided for any decision to be unanimously accepted. Angus and the core of the English party remained loyal to Henry, and they were now joined by Lennox, who was of necessity on the other side from his dynastic rival Arran. Lennox left Stirling almost immediately after the Queen's coronation and made for Dumbarton, where he met envoys from France who brought money, artillery, and munitions, and also the patriarch of Aquileia, who came from the Pope to collect the last ecclesiastical subsidy solicited by the late king. The newcomers, who were unaware of Lennox's change of front, handed over to him the supplies they had brought, and the pro-English faction took up arms, despite an over-ingenious proposal by Beaton for all-round conciliation: according to this, Arran was to be divorced and marry the Dowager Queen, and Lennox, a man of twenty-six but a bachelor, was to be contracted to the infant Mary.

Henry could not accept the repudiation by the Scots of the marriage treaty, and his calculation that he had secured his northern frontier while he went to war with France had been disappointed. To make matters worse, the Emperor deserted him in 1544, leaving him to face France alone, and preparations were being made for the Council of Trent, which met in the following year to provide a rallying point for papalist activity which might be directed against England. He therefore renewed his understanding with Lennox, Angus, Cassillis, and Glencairn, who undertook to cause the Word of God to be preached in Scotland, to endeavour to have Mary put into Henry's hands, and to have him made Protector of Scotland during her minority. But the military operations of this party were a failure and Henry returned to the policy of direct force from England. In May 1544 he sent north an army under the Earl of Hertford with instructions to do the maximum damage; Hertford took the

Scots by surprise and was able to disembark one force near Edinburgh, while another came overland, and together they spread devastation throughout south-eastern Scotland, giving particular attention to the religious houses, which derived less protection than ever from their sacred character now that the English had dissolved their own monasteries. Lennox had meantime made his way to England. There he improved his position by marrying Margaret Douglas, who was the daughter of Margaret Tudor by the Earl of Angus and who stood next to Queen Mary in the line of succession to the English throne, and Henry proclaimed him Lieutenant for northern England and southern Scotland. He conducted various military operations, with little success.

It did not improve matters for the Scots that what may be called the national party was itself divided. The administration headed by Arran and Beaton was discredited by the easy successes of Hertford and by its own severities against heretics. Therefore an attempt was made in the summer of 1544 to supersede Arran as Governor by Mary of Guise, in whom there may well have been more confidence. Mary showed considerable skill, now as later, in winning notables to her side and especially in coming to terms with at least some of the lords of the English faction, but her supporters hardly formed a party, for they had no real political platform to differentiate their policy from Beaton's. However, the caballings which went on had at least the effect of temporarily detaching Angus and his following from Henry. One element was simple finance. Henry had been making offers of £100 or £200 to Scottish nobles in 1543, but the Scottish government, with some French backing, made counterbids. In a competitive market, prices rose, for in May 1544 the English offered Glencairn £1,000, while in December Angus received a Scottish pension of £1,000, and the Earl of Bothwell another of the same amount. The Scottish government succeeded in outbidding Henry, and at the end of the year there was something like a coalition, on the plea of unity against 'our auld inymeis of England'. The policy adopted, and maintained as long as Beaton lived, was essentially a compromise, for although some help in money and men came from France, French influence did not predominate. Queen Mary was kept in Scotland; there was so much repugnance to her marriage abroad that Arran gained increasing support for her betrothal to his son; and in the continuing military operations against England it was the erstwhile English agent Angus who led the Scots to victory at Ancrum in February 1545.

This was all totally unacceptable to England, but Henry had no new policy. When the Scots refused to reopen negotiations on the basis of the Treaties of Greenwich, he launched another invasion. Hertford came up again in September 1545, a season deliberately chosen as suitable for the burning of crops cut in an early harvest. Lennox resumed activities in the Firth of Clyde and Henry succeeded, as many of his predecessors had done, in winning the support of several of the leading west-Highland chiefs, who consented to something like an English-sponsored administration in their area. The figurehead of the administration was soon killed, and as there was no agreement about a successor the movement petered out, while Lennox made little more impression now than he had done earlier. The English invasions, which are together known as the 'Rough Wooing' and were in a sense an action for breach of promise, look like the negation of statesmanship, for they rather had the effect of antagonizing even Scots who were in principle in favour of amity with England. Nor had Henry's bribery of Scottish nobles produced any noticeable results. One good stroke, however, was done in his favour: the elimination of Cardinal Beaton.

Beaton had made himself unpopular on several counts. The foreign policy he advocated had led to the 'Rough Wooing' and the administration he supported had shown itself unable to protect the people of south-eastern Scotland from the consequent suffering. To those who cared for the wellbeing of the Church he represented much that was bad: he was a pluralist, with as many titles 'as would have loaded a ship, much less an ass', he had a large family whom he endowed with ecclesiastical property, he was immersed in affairs of state, and he was an active persecutor of heretics. Besides, he would appear to have

been on bad terms with some of his neighbours in Fife, where
lairds were in any event inclined to be pro-English and pro-
Reformation. Henry VIII, who rightly saw Beaton as the principal obstacle to his schemes in Scotland, had little difficulty in
finding agents who would try to encompass the cardinal's death.
It is not, however, clear whether it was English promptings
which led directly to the cardinal's assassination in his castle
of St Andrews on 29 May 1546, though some of the murderers
had been parties to Henry's plots.

Beaton's fate is always linked with that of George Wishart,
whom he had put to death for heresy three months earlier
(1 March). Wishart, after spending some time at Cambridge, had
returned to Scotland in 1543 in company with the English commissioners sent to negotiate the Treaties of Greenwich. He was
clearly a political agent as well as a preacher of the Gospel,
but there is no proof that he was identical with the 'Scottish
man called Wishart' who was involved in plots against the
cardinal, and reformers saw in him an innocent victim of
Beaton's cruelty. His execution certainly intensified resentment,
and the Fife lairds who broke into St Andrews Castle to murder
the cardinal represented their action as one of vengeance and
indeed of justice.

> James Melville (a man of nature most gentle and most modest)
> . . . said, 'This work and judgment of God (although it be secret)
> ought to be done with greater gravity'; and presenting unto him the
> point of the sword, said, 'Repent thee of thy former wicked life, but
> especially of the shedding of the blood of that notable instrument
> of God, Master George Wishart.'

The murderers retained possession of the castle, on a promon-
tory jutting into the North Sea, and asked for English assistance
in return for their readiness to further the English marriage
project. When it was thought that they would obtain English
help they were joined by John Knox, a priest who had been
associated with Wishart and who was now accepted as a
preacher. However, while they received money and some encouragement from England, armed help was not forthcoming.

Yet Arran could not retake the castle by his own resources: he
may have been inept, but it was a difficulty that his son, previously a compulsory guest of the cardinal, was now a hostage
in the hands of the 'Castilians', who might hand him over to
Henry. At any rate, it was only with French help that the castle
was invested and ultimately taken (31 July 1547). The most
important of the Castilians were imprisoned in France, while the
rank and file, including Knox, were consigned to the galleys,
where Knox remained until 1549.

England, too late to save her friends in St Andrews, acted
later in the year. Scotland's old scourge Hertford, now Duke of
Somerset and Protector of England under the young Edward
VI, brought up a strong force which the Scots met at Pinkie
(10 September). The Scots had a large army – perhaps too large,
for it included men among whom there could be little mutual
confidence. The clergy, who regarded the campaign as a crusade,
brought a banner which entreated God to have mercy on His
afflicted spouse, the Church; and a considerable number of
churchmen fell in the battle. Arran may have seen things in the
same light, but it is unlikely that there was much confidence in
his leadership, and it is hard to believe that Angus, who led the
van, cared much for either Arran or the clergy. An element of
distrust in the Scottish ranks may have done much to bring
about the confusion and panic which led to complete disaster.
England followed up the victory not by attempting the conquest of Scotland, but by planting garrisons in a number of
strongpoints in south-eastern Scotland and as far north as
Broughty Castle, near Dundee. Their main centre was Haddington, from which they could control East Lothian and threaten
the whole country up to Edinburgh, only seventeen miles away.

Somerset had been pushing propaganda in favour of an English
alliance and that 'godly and honourable purpose' the English
marriage, and his troops found much support. The people of
the south-east, while they had less reason than ever to love the
English, had every reason to fear them, and must have weighed
afresh the benefits to their security and economy which would
flow from peace. Religious motives, however, were even

stronger. Each English garrison was a centre of Protestant influence, and less than two months after Pinkie the English governor of Broughty reported that there was much desire in Angus
and Fife for Bibles and Testaments and 'other good English
books'. One thoughtful Scot, puzzled to find the explanation
why the Scottish government was not obeyed and the English
were favoured, could find four 'principal causes', and, while
three of them were material – the desire for security, for profit,
and for stable government – he gave first place to the fact that
'part of the lieges have taken new opinions of the Scripture and
have done against the law and ordinance of Holy Church'. While
the motives might be diverse, the fact was that, once the occu-
pation was over, hundreds of Scots were found guilty of 'taking
of assurance with our old enemies of England, fortifying and
assistance giving to them'.

A government of such a divided nation, a government which
had been unable to resist, far less to repel, successive English
invasions, and which had been unable even to capture St
Andrews Castle without help, could hardly by its own efforts
drive the English from the points which they occupied. France
was the obvious source of support, for France was at war with
England and it would be useful to her to exert pressure on
England from the north. But the French would not act except on
conditions. As Arran had forfeited all confidence not only by his
incompetence but by his unashamed attempts to advance his
own kinsmen, he had no choice but to come to terms. He had
already released from their undertaking those who had promised
to further the marriage of Mary to his son, and he was attracted
by the offer of a daughter of the Duke of Montpensier in her
place. He had presumably been making free with the vast fortune left by James V, and he obtained an agreement that no
questions would be asked about his financial operations as governor. In January 1548 he promised that, in return for a French
duchy, he would secure the consent of the Scottish parliament
to the marriage of Mary to the Dauphin, her removal to France,
and the delivery of Scottish strongholds into French hands. In
short, Scotland could escape from English domination only at

the cost of submitting to French domination, and the Scottish Queen, once destined to be the bride of the heir of England, was now to be the bride of the heir of France. A French force soon arrived, and a joint Franco-Scottish army laid siege to the principal English stronghold, Haddington. There, on 7 July 1548, a treaty was made whereby it was agreed that Mary should marry the Dauphin but that Scotland should retain its own liberties and laws.

Mary had been sheltered from danger in her infancy and girlhood, and those troubled years can have meant nothing to her. She was mainly at Stirling, but at the time of Hertford's first invasion she was reported to have been taken to Dunkeld, and during the Pinkie campaign she spent three weeks in the safety of the island priory of Inchmahome, west of Stirling. In July 1548 the fleet which had landed French forces at Leith sailed round to Dumbarton, where the Queen and her four Maries – Beaton, Seton, Fleming, and Livingston – were taken on board. After waiting for a favourable wind and then making a circuit by the west of Ireland, the ships reached Roscoff, near Brest, on 13 August, but may have gone on to St Pol and landed the passengers there on 15 August. Some weeks earlier Arran's son and heir had also been shipped to France; by this time almost a professional hostage, he was again a pledge for his father's good behaviour.

The Scots had to be reconciled to the reaffirmation of the French alliance, about which some of them had long had doubts. While Arran was satisfied with the duchy of Châtelherault, worth 12,000 livres a year, conferred on him in February 1549, and the promotion of his half-brother, John, to the archbishopric of St Andrews in June, the consent of other Scots had to be secured as well. Angus and Huntly, besides Arran, were admitted to the Order of St Michael, but more material inducements or rewards were also necessary. In 1550 Mary of Guise went to France with a remarkable train, nearly all of them men who had been committed, or at least inclined, to the English and reforming side. The visit has been called a 'brain-washing expedition', but France worked on their pockets as well as their

1 Linlithgow Palace and Church

11 The Château of Chambord

brains. It was reported that the King of France 'bought them completely', and this generalization is borne out by the evidence that the Earl of Glencairn, Lords Home and Maxwell, and the Master of Ruthven became French pensioners and that two of Mary's half-brothers – James, Commendator of St Andrews, and John, Commendator of Coldingham – were nominated to French abbeys.

At some stage the management of Scotland and the appeasement of Scots took on a new complexion, for the task came to be not only to reconcile the country to the consequences of the Treaty of Haddington – the proposed marriage of Mary in France and the presence in Scotland of several French garrisons – but to carry through a softening-up process designed to pave the way for the acceptance of Mary of Guise as Governor in place of Arran. Already when the Queen Mother was in France, in February 1551, it was rumoured that the French meant to 'prevene [anticipate] the time of the Governor's office before the Queen's coming to perfect age'. In practice, D'Oysel, the French resident in Scotland, was said to exercise almost sovereign authority, and French representatives took it on themselves to act for Scotland in her relations with both England and the Emperor. There was a danger that Arran's governorship might become little more than camouflage.

But the Scots were clearly restive, for the French troops in Scotland were, as ever, unpopular, the lieges had become more than weary of the incessant musters, and in 1552, when France and the Emperor were again at war, it was impossible to prevail on Scotland to resume hostilities or even to raise a Scottish force for service in the French army. Significantly enough, at this point parliament passed an Act which in effect ratified Arran's legal position as Governor. While his freedom of action was curbed by the fact that his son was in France, there are some indications of a policy which might have brought support from England, still under the Protestant government of Edward VI. In 1549 and 1552 the Governor's brother John, Archbishop of St Andrews, held councils of the Scottish Church to pass a whole code of statutes designed to reform abuses and to approve a Catechism which, in its teaching on Justification and the Eucharist, went some way towards satisfying the reformers. Besides, with John Hamilton as Archbishop and Legate *a latēre* and his brother as Governor, the Pope (who was not mentioned in the Catechism) was being quietly bowed out of the direction of Scottish church affairs, and a kind of Hamiltonian papacy paralleled the Henrician papacy which had taken shape earlier in England. The statutes of the reforming councils might appeal to those who sought the welfare of the Church, they might weaken the Protestant opposition, and, as nothing was said about ecclesiastical endowments, they did not, as more thorough-going reforms would have done, alienate the nobles and lairds who already had their hands on so much of the Church's wealth. At the same time, they groomed the Scottish administration to make it look attractive to Protestant England. In 1553 it was actually rumoured that Arran had asked for the assistance of the King of England 'on the ground of the new religion'. As long as Edward reigned in England, Arran, however impotent in reality, must remain nominally Governor of Scotland.

The cue for Arran's removal came with the death of Edward VI (6 July 1553), the accession of Mary, daughter of Catherine of Aragon, and the prospect that England would soon be reconciled to Rome. English help could not now be expected for an anti-French party in Scotland which would necessarily be also anti-papal. Little time was lost, for in December 1553 the *parlement* of Paris declared its opinion that Mary, who had only entered and not completed her twelfth year, was of 'perfect age' and entitled to choose a Governor: this was the equivalent of the change, in private law, from 'tutory' to 'curatory', which was understood in Scotland to take place when a girl completed her twelfth year. However, no decision of a French *parlement* was binding in Scotland, and the course which was followed there was one which amounted to buying the Hamiltons out by a series of financial concessions. There was a reaffirmation of the understanding that no questions were to be asked about Châtel-herault's intromissions with crown revenues and of the expectation that his eldest son would marry a French lady of high rank. On 9 December Archbishop Hamilton (who already had another Hamilton, Gavin, as coadjutor) resigned the abbey of Paisley, which was granted to the duke's fourth son, Claude, and two days later the papal bulls providing the duke's second son, John, to the wealthy abbey of Arbroath were executed. The archbishop resigned the office of Treasurer of the Realm in return for an assignation to him of the arrears, amounting to £31,000, and a series of gifts. On 1 March 1554 Mary of Guise gave an assurance that Scotland would continue to be governed by its own laws and customs and that the duke's family were to succeed to the throne failing issue of the Queen. In April 1554 parliament formally transferred the regency to the Queen Mother, but was emphatic that the transaction had taken place 'before the Queen's perfect age'. No one can have had much respect for the deposed Governor, and it was even said that all the lords of Scotland were against him, yet it was felt that he had been swindled out of his rights, and John Knox, who had never forgiven Arran for his desertion of the reforming cause in 1543, said that he had been removed from office 'justly by God but most unjustly by men'.

Such an action was perhaps not a very promising beginning for an administration which was bound to pursue a policy shaped by the interests of France and therefore unpopular in Scotland, and it says much for Mary of Guise that she managed to maintain her position for more than five years. Her methods were diverse, but in the main they were along the lines of conciliation, which was always the key to the successful government of Scotland. By the skilful use of crown patronage, gifts were made as judiciously as they had been by Cardinal Beaton when he was countering Henry VIII's offers. For example, something was done to wean the Campbell Earl of Argyll from his attachment to the Reformation by recommending a Campbell for the bishopric of Brechin; the Earl of Glencairn, a devotee of the Protestant cause, was designated for a pension of £900 from the abbey of Kelso; by some means a bond was secured whereby the Earl of Morton, another incipient Protestant, pledged his support; the Earl of Cassillis, who had been one of the lords selected to accompany the Dowager on the brain-washing trip to France in 1550, was chosen to succeed John Hamilton as Treasurer. The penalties imposed on lesser men who had been conspicuous as anglophiles in the 1540s were now revoked. Mary also established a relationship of understanding and confidence with some of the merchants and burghs.

So far as the progress of reforming opinions was concerned, it may be doubted if a return to ecclesiastical discipline, except by the use of force such as no Scottish government possessed, was any longer practicable, and it had been remarked as early as 1547 that 'heresy is now doubtsome to punish by the law'. Probably effective control had never recovered from the shock of 1543, when the vernacular Bible was authorized and there had been attacks on religious houses; the English invasions, which wrecked the fabric of the south-eastern abbeys, must have harmed their community life as well; Beaton's murder, apart from its intrinsic significance, had been the signal for fresh attacks on ecclesiastical properties; and Hamilton's reforming councils must have suggested that further pressure might bring yet more concessions. At any rate the official policy was one of remarkable leniency, and, while it would be an injustice to see in Mary of Guise one who was by temperament a zealot or a persecutor, there were ulterior motives. As long as Mary Tudor was pursuing her Romanizing policy in England, Scottish Protestants did not represent a political danger, since they had no English backing; besides, if reformers could preach with impunity in Scotland they might encourage English Protestants and weaken Mary Tudor's government. One of those who thus preached was John Willock, who had actually been associated with a rebellion against Mary Tudor in 1554; another was John Knox, who had gone to Geneva after Mary Tudor's accession and was something of a leader of left-wing English Protestantism. Mary of Guise's tolerance of course influenced only the civil government, and the ecclesiastical authorities might have taken a different line. But at the head of the hierarchy was John Hamilton, ever careful of the interests of his house, which he could not afford to injure by a display of severity. In a situation where the heads of Church and State were in competition to court the Protestants, a reformed organization began to develop without interference.

If leniency and conciliation meant the growth of a movement which was bound, in the long run, to be subversive, it was also true that all the Dowager's amiability was urgently needed, for other policies she had to pursue were highly unpopular. Frenchmen in Scotland had never enjoyed cordial relations with the native Scots, and friction with the French soldiers was intensified at this point because delay in paying their wages led to relaxed discipline. Not only were there French garrisons, but Frenchmen were thrust into political offices. Thus De Roubay was Vice-Chancellor and in effect superseded Huntly, the Chancellor; Villemore, a former member of the Queen Mother's household, became Comptroller; John Roytell was Master of Works. Behind and above them there was still D'Oysel, the resident French ambassador, who continued to be influential. This was not only an affront to national sentiment, but deprived Scottish notables of positions which they thought their due. As early as 1555 an Act had to be passed against 'speaking evil of the Queen's grace and of Frenchmen'.

With the marriage of Mary Tudor to Philip of Spain, arranged in January 1554 and celebrated in July, England was a satellite of the Hapsburgs, and France was more anxious than ever to use Scotland as a base. There was a phase when the war on the Continent went badly for the French, with a Spanish victory at St Quentin in August 1557 which led to a threat to Paris itself. Thereafter, however, the French took the offensive in campaigns which ultimately captured Calais, the last relic of England's attempts to conquer France. The complementary stroke would be to mount an attack from the north against Berwick, the last relic of her attempts to conquer Scotland. At one time the Scots would have rallied eagerly to retake Berwick, but now the recovery of that town (which had not been in their hands since 1482) was evidently no inducement. Instead, they felt that they were being expected to contribute to military operations which represented French aggression against England rather than the

defence of Scotland against a power which did not at that time
seem to constitute any threat, and the government encountered afresh the reluctance of Scottish nobles to 'hazard battle
furth of their own country'. The attitude of the Borderers in
particular may have caused much recrimination. They had no
objection to a state of war which in a sense legalized their thiev-
ing habits, but they had a fellow-feeling for their English opposite numbers and preferred to conduct proceedings as little more
than a kind of rough game in which few people were seriously
hurt. The French may well have complained that it was not
possible to wage war without casualties. The traditional levies
were inadequate and unreliable for the kind of campaigns the
French had in mind, and money had therefore to be sought to
pay 'wagers' or hired soldiers who could serve for long periods,
as well as for expensive fortifications; a fort at Kelso, for
example, was going to cost £20,000.

Mary applied to the Pope for a subvention from the Church,
and even suggested that as monasteries had outlived their use-
fulness their wealth might now be at the disposal of the State.
The Pope did concede a tax of one-twentieth in 1556 and again
in 1557, but he was less impressed than Clement VII had been
when Scotland was an instrument against Henry VIII, for he
cannot have felt much enthusiasm for subsidizing attacks on his
faithful daughter Mary Tudor. In desperation for funds, the
government made a startling proposal in 1556 for a perpetual
tax to be raised on a new assessment not only of lands but of
every person's 'substance and goods movable and immovable'.
While everyone in the social scale was involved, the nobles
naturally led the opposition and withstood the proposal, 'affirming that they meant not to put their goods in inventory, as if
they were to make their last wills and testaments'. This great
tax was never levied, but the suggestion must have undermined
confidence in the government, and the taxes which were imposed were collected only with 'danger, grudge, or murmur of
the people'. Resentment against France and against a government acting in the French interest reinforced the other factors

which had led to the growth of a pro-English party, and it was probably decisive in making that party prevail.

The Dauphin, Francis, would become legally of age to marry on his fourteenth birthday in January 1558, and this long-awaited date now determined the timetable of French policy. On 30 October 1557 Henry II had written to the Scottish estates intimating that he proposed that the marriage should be contracted on 16 January next and requesting them to send commissioners to France to conclude the marriage terms. On 14 December the estates appointed the necessary commission, which agreed to the marriage but – out of deference to the laws of Scotland as well as to a specific protest by Châtelherault for his right of succession – secured a recognition of the claims of the Scottish heirs should Francis and Mary have no issue. The marriage took place at Notre Dame on 24 April 1558. Mary and Francis had taken to each other as young children and a real affection had developed between the vivacious girl and a boy who was sickly, feeble and stunted physically and timid and diffident in his nature – a relationship of admiration on his side, sympathy and protection on hers. But it is very doubtful if the puny Francis had reached adulthood, either physically or emotionally, even by the time he died, two and a half years after the marriage, and there is no question of mature passion.

Both before and after the marriage, safeguards for Scotland were several times affirmed. On 15 April Mary pledged herself and her successors to observe the laws, liberties, and privileges of Scotland; on 19 April, Francis and she issued a declaration in similar terms and added expressly that should Mary die without issue the nearest heir would succeed to the Scottish crown; on 30 April, six days after the marriage, Francis and Mary, now styled 'King and Queen of Scots' as well as Dauphin and Dauphiness, repeated the intention to preserve Scottish laws and liberties; and on 26 June Francis made a separate declaration of similar tenor. If any contemporary thought they protested too much he was amply justified, for on 4 April, three weeks before her marriage, Mary had signed three documents which completely nullified all those safeguards for her ancient kingdom and its rightful heirs. She bequeathed Scotland to the King of France failing issue of her marriage, put her kingdom in pledge to him for sums spent on its defence and on her education, and annulled any promises which might be made contrary to the first and second undertakings. It was not without reason that the French believed that by the marriage the sovereignty of Scotland had simply been transferred to the French royal house. When four out of the eight Scottish commissioners who had been sent to France died before they were out of that country, the suspicion was raised that they had learned, or guessed, too much.

The French may well have calculated that trouble would arise from the inconsistency between the public and the private declarations. It appears that the commissioners themselves were pressed to arrange for the Scottish crown to be sent to France so that Francis could be crowned with it, and that they refused. Later in the year, on 29 November, the Scottish parliament did consent that Francis should be honoured with 'the crown matrimonial', but made it clear that this was not to imply a transference of the Scottish succession to the heirs of Francis should he outlive Mary and have children by another wife. Even if contemporaries in Scotland were not aware of Mary's duplicity and of French attitudes, the prospect they saw for their country was a bleak one. They did not know as we do that Francis would die less than three years after his marriage, leaving Mary a childless widow; the likelihood was that he would live, that Mary and he would have a son who would inherit both countries, and that Scotland would simply be merged into one dominion under the French Crown.

To reconcile Scots to this prospect was bound to tax Mary of Guise's diplomatic skill to the utmost. Three friends to the Reformation had been among the eight commissioners sent to France, and the reformers were permitted to press their advantage in a favourable situation. For a time there had been divided counsels among them. In the spring of 1557 some Protestant lords had asked John Knox to come back again from Geneva, but later the invitation was cancelled, to the indignation of

Knox, who had reached Dieppe when he was told to come no further. Equally, a bond drawn up in December 1557, pledging its signatories to forsake the 'congregation of Antichrist' and to work, as the congregation of Christ, for the establishment of a reformed Church, seems to have gained far less support than was expected. But early in 1558, the 'lords and barons professing Christ Jesus' drew up proposals for reformed worship and went on not only to organize congregations in a number of places but also to petition for public services in the vernacular and for the reform of the lives of the clergy. Archbishop Hamilton was now beginning to feel that the situation was getting out of hand, but the Governor directed him to summon yet another provincial council, which met in March and April 1559. It was not prepared for radical changes, but it passed another batch of well-intentioned statutes against abuses and it authorized the issue to communicants of a 'Godly Exhortation' which in its general tenor resembled the exhortations which had appeared in the first instalment of liturgical reform in England, the Order of Communion of 1548.

This was the end of the policy of conciliation, for changes in the political situation made it possible for the Scottish government to take up the challenge presented by the reformers. Mary Tudor died on 17 November 1558 and this broke the close link between England and Spain. The new Queen, who had been born to Anne Boleyn while the Pope still refused to annul Henry VIII's marriage to Catherine of Aragon, could hardly be a papalist, and it was soon evident that there would be ecclesiastical changes in England. Besides, as Roman Catholics denied Elizabeth's legitimacy, Mary and Francis assumed the style and arms of sovereigns of England. England, which had lost Calais in January 1558, was more than ever apprehensive about Berwick and was left without an ally when Spain and France came to terms in the Treaty of Cateau-Cambrésis (March–April 1559). Not only might Elizabeth's new and insecure government have to face, in isolation, an attack by France, using Scotland as a base from which to assert the claim of Mary to the English throne, but Spain also might be brought into a crusade against her.

France, on her side, having already gained Calais and being now freed from the Spanish threat, had no need to woo the Scots as a distraction to England, and since Francis and Mary were now husband and wife there was no need to court the Scots to gain their assent to that union. Therefore Mary of Guise, probably under direction from France, turned on the reformers just as Henry II turned on the Huguenots in France. Knox says that from Easter 1559 (26 March) she 'appeared altogether altered'. Yet the reformers were taking the initiative in a way which no government could have ignored, and they must bear the main responsibility for the troubles which followed. Already in the previous summer there were the first signs of disaffection in the capital, for the statue of St Giles was destroyed and a riot broke out when a substitute was later carried in procession. About the end of the year the 'Beggars' Summons' had been posted on the doors of friaries, warning the inmates to quit their houses at the next Whitsunday term. But it is doubtful if a revolution could have been carried through against the Dowager and her standing army without English intervention, and perhaps the most important development was the re-emergence of a *rapprochement* between the Scottish dissidents and the English, which had been impossible since the accession of Mary Tudor in 1553. In January 1559 Châtelherault was con-ferring with Sir Henry Percy on the Borders and the negotiations for the Treaty of Cateau-Cambrésis gave an opportunity to William Maitland of Lethington, the Scottish Secretary, to estab-lish contacts with English diplomats.

Faced with the Dowager's patent hostility and encouraged by the prospect of English help, the reformers prepared for militant action. The kernel of unrest was the 'godly town' of Dundee, with its outstanding record of adherence to reform; and its burgesses, as well as those of the nearby town of Perth, now publicly embraced the Reformation. When the Governor replied by summoning the Protestant preachers to appear before her at Stirling on 10 May, the burgesses of Perth and Dundee and the gentlemen of Angus mustered in their defence. It was at this juncture that John Knox arrived again. After seeking in vain for admission to England, he had landed at Leith on 2 May and then made for the trouble centre. On 11 May, in St John's church at Perth, he preached a sermon which led to a riot in which church ornaments and furnishings were destroyed and the houses of the Carthusian monks and the Dominican and Franciscan friars were despoiled. The looting continued on the 12th, which was 'Flitting Friday', the Friday preceding Whitsunday and therefore the day on which, according to the Beggars' Summons, the friars were expected to remove. The dissidents made it clear that they would resist attempts at suppression, for they appealed by letter to 'all brethren' and, to anticipate a muster called by the government at Stirling for 24 May, 'the brethren from all quarters' came flocking into Perth.

This meant civil war, and military operations, largely inconclusive and often half-hearted, went on for more than a year. There was something of a landslide of Scottish support away from the Governor, and D'Oysel complained, 'You cannot tell friend from enemy, and he who is with us in the morning is on the other side after dinner.' But Mary of Guise retained a standing army of French professionals which could keep the field while the forces of 'the Congregation', volunteers and ill-paid, were apt to melt away. In June and July, as the insurgents advanced from Perth to Stirling, Linlithgow, and Edinburgh, the Regent had to retire to Dunbar, but by the end of July she was back in Leith and Holyrood, while Edinburgh was declared neutral territory. Meantime, by the death of Henry II (10 July), Francis and Mary were King and Queen of France as well as of Scotland, and this facilitated the co-ordination of French and Scottish policy. In August and September about 2,000 more troops arrived, giving the Dowager probably 4,000 men.

The insurgents' best prospect, if not their only hope, lay in winning similar help from England. The accession of Francis in France might have been expected to alienate England from France, for the Queen Consort of France, as she now was, had not renounced her claim to England. On the other hand, it was now less likely that Mary would ever want to return to Scotland and, if she were faced with a revolution there, she might be ready to relinquish her rights. What was pointed to was an understanding between England and the Scottish revolutionaries and a plan for the deposition of Mary. Cecil, Elizabeth's minister, was quite ready for this, but his mistress was slow to move, for she had a natural antipathy to rebellion against lawful sovereigns and, although she sent the Scots £3,000 in August 1559, she decided that she could not afford military action. Nor did Knox improve matters by exhorting her to 'forget your birth and all title which thereupon doth hang'. But there were difficulties on the Scottish side as well, for many Scots who were anti-French and anti-papal were nonetheless disinclined to depose their Queen; besides, should Mary be deposed, who was to succeed, when the claims were canvassed of both her half-brother, Lord James (since 1557 the eldest surviving bastard of James V), and the heir presumptive, Châtelherault? The latter cannot have been a popular candidate, and had not yet committed himself to the revolutionary cause, for his hands were tied as long as his son was still a hostage in France; on the other hand, the elevation of a royal bastard to the throne would have been startlingly novel.

Elizabeth, who would not send an army and was on the whole unlikely to countenance Moray – though many thought she was a bastard herself – was brought round to cultivate Châtelherault. This made it essential to engineer his son's escape. Young Arran, whose long-deferred hopes of marrying Mary seemed to have been finally extinguished by her marriage to Francis, had adopted the reformed religion in France and was ready enough to come to terms with England, especially as it was evident that, should the Scottish crown pass to the Hamiltons, he was an obvious husband for Elizabeth. The appearance of an English ambassador in Paris in May, following the conclusion of peace at Cateau-Cambrésis, opened a channel of communication, and through his agency Arran's escape was arranged in June. At this time there were alarming reports about Mary's health, and Henry II, seeing that Scotland might slip from his grasp if she died, tried to secure Arran. On finding him already gone from his residence, he ordered the Channel ports to be watched, but English agents arranged a circuitous journey by way of Geneva and Friesland. Arran, brought secretly to Cecil's house in London on 28 August, had an interview with Elizabeth, but she did not commit herself on the subject of marriage. As soon as the duke learned that Arran was on the way home, he began to negotiate with the Lords of the Congregation, and on 19 September, three days after his son reached Stirling, he formally joined them. The duke's brother John, the archbishop, adhered to Mary of Guise, but Gavin Hamilton, his coadjutor, followed the duke into the opposite camp: the Hamiltons' prospects were thus taken care of, whatever the outcome.

Now that the insurgents had the heir presumptive as a figurehead, they resumed the offensive both militarily and politically. They marched on Edinburgh and, after an ultimatum demanding that the Regent should desist from turning Leith into a strongly fortified base, 'suspended' her from authority (21 October). The action was taken in the name of the absent King and Queen and on the ground of the Dowager's actions in introducing fresh French troops, fortifying Leith, and in general ignoring the advice of the 'born councillors' of the realm.

But the military situation was soon a stalemate which there was no possibility of resolving by Scottish effort alone. The provisional government found it hard to raise money, and funds on their way to them from England were intercepted by the Earl of Bothwell, with the result that their troops again began to disband, and, after a failure in an attack on Leith, they had to retreat in disorder to Stirling. They might reassemble an army, but the French could again fall back on Leith, which was impregnable except to artillery which the Scots did not have at their disposal. On the other hand, while the French could not conquer Scotland, they could remain in Leith and await reinforcements from France. Maitland of Lethington was sent south to urge Elizabeth to come to the rescue. Meantime the French were able to take the offensive: they drove the insur-

gents from Stirling and, from their bases at Leith and on the
island of Inchkeith in the Firth of Forth, began operations in
Fife which drove the rebels before them. Mary of Guise is
alleged to have exclaimed at this point, 'Where is now John
Knox's God? My God is stronger than his, yea, even in Fife.'
The situation was saved by the appearance of an English fleet
in the Firth of Forth in January 1560, ostensibly to seek out
pirates, in reality to cut communications between the French
base at Leith and both Fife and France. The French forces in
Fife had to withdraw by way of Stirling, and the reforming
party was saved from annihilation.

But intervention from England by land was necessary if the
French were to be driven to relinquish their hold on Scotland. On
22 February Scottish commissioners representing Châtelherault
and the lords associated with him 'for maintenance and defence
of the ancient rights and liberties of the country' made a treaty
at Berwick with the Duke of Norfolk, Lieutenant of the North
of England. This treaty represented the policy of Elizabeth and
of Maitland of Lethington rather than of Knox or of those who
had thought of deposing Mary. There was no hint that religion
was an issue; Châtelherault and his associates were not to withdraw their obedience from their lawful sovereigns, provided
that the liberties of the subjects were not infringed; England,
on her side, agreed to intervene for the preservation of the Scots
'in their old freedom and liberties' and to give them protection
for the duration of Mary's marriage and for a year thereafter.

English troops entered Scotland at the end of March and
pressed the siege of Leith with their artillery, but the French
put up a stubborn resistance and, although they were reduced
to famine, reinforcements and supplies might yet reach them
from France. However, a French fleet was scattered by a storm
in January, and political and religious troubles then in effect
neutralized France. Two French envoys made their way through
England, to mediate in Scotland, and they were joined by English
representatives, Sir William Cecil and Dr Nicholas Wotton.
While their discussions were going on, the Queen Regent, who
had retired to Edinburgh Castle on 1 April, died on 11 June: as

she had shown no readiness to negotiate except on condition
that the rebels returned to their obedience, and it was hard to
see what place she could have in any settlement which recognized a Scottish revolution, she displayed 'exquisite tact' by
dying 'at the very time when her death removed the last obstacle to peace'. On 6 July, at Edinburgh, a treaty was concluded between the English and French commissioners. In brief,
both English and French troops were to withdraw from Scotland
and Mary was to cease 'henceforward' to use the arms of
England with their implied claim to Elizabeth's throne. The
removal of foreign armies was to leave the Scots free to settle
their own affairs, and among 'Concessions' granted in the name
of the King and Queen it was provided that a parliament should
be summoned and the country administered by a council con-
sisting of seven or eight members chosen by Mary and five or
six by the estates.

The fighting had been mainly between English and French
and it seems that little Scottish blood had been shed. This was
not only characteristic of the Scots, who, while they might differ
in principle, were singularly lacking in personal animosity
against each other, but also significant of the underlying fact
that the Scottish revolution was a mere incident in an international struggle. Against the background of the previous half
century, it was quite appropriate that the future of Scotland
should be decided by a treaty made between England and France.

But if there had been little bloodshed among the Scots there
had been plenty of argument. The case presented by the insurgents in 1559 had been designed to appeal to patriotic resentment
against the French rather than to religion. Already in June they
claimed that national integrity had been threatened by the marriage of Mary and Francis, and the arrival in August of additional
French troops, accompanied by their families, gave more specific
grounds for alarm. Frenchmen, it was said, were to be planted
in the 'native rooms' or landed possessions of Scots, while the
'just possessors and ancient inhabitants' were to be rejected;
and the Earl of Argyll, after remarking that the French 'are
come in and sitten down in this realm to occupy it and to put

forth the inhabitants thereof', went on to 'make the example of Britanny', which had been absorbed into France through marriage earlier in the century. An appeal was made to one peer for his support on the ground of 'the common weal and liberty of this your native country', although he might not be 'resolute towards the religion'. Mary of Guise retorted to this propaganda by accusing the opposition of aiming at the overthrow of 'the authority' and the transfer of the crown from her daughter, and this made an impression on many conservative Scots. Besides, the Congregation's new ally, Elizabeth, did not take kindly to any threats to the rights of princes. Consequently, the lords began to protest that they contended only for 'the Evangel' and did not aim at 'inobedience of the prince or usurping of higher powers', and in 1560 they began to put more emphasis on religious objectives. This won wider support; the burgh of Aberdeen agreed to support 'the Congregation' provided that it did not 'enterprise any purpose against the authority', and a new bond, pledging support for the reformation of religion and the end of French domination, but affirming obedience to the lawful sovereigns, was acceptable to the Earl of Huntly, who was probably of one mind with the loyal burgesses of Aberdeen.

When the withdrawal of foreign armies left the Scots free to settle their own affairs, any idea of a political revolution was quietly dropped. The insurgent administration had already decided in May that a parliament should be proclaimed for July, and the 'Concessions' granted at the time of the Treaty of Edinburgh expressly authorized a parliament, which met in August. The restrictions imposed in those 'Concessions' seem, however, to have been ignored, for the existing administration remained in control, and the parliament, both in its composition and in its work, paid no heed to the wishes of the sovereigns. According to the 'Concessions' the meeting was to be one at which it was to be lawful 'for all those to be present who are in use to be present'; this clause may have been designed to prevent the exclusion of the prelates, and bishops were in fact present, but the gathering also included a large number of lairds who were certainly not 'in use to be present'. Again, the parliament had been forbidden to deal with religion, which was to be referred to the King and Queen; but it did deal with religion, in Acts which accepted a reformed Confession of Faith, abrogated papal authority, and forbade the celebration of Mass. In the 'Concessions' it had been declared that the proposed parliament would be as valid as if it had been called by Francis and Mary in person, but such validity could not extend to a parliament which violated other terms in the 'Concessions'.

The parliament probably went as far as it could in such an uncertain situation. The legislation was certainly in some respects minimal reformation, for nothing was said about the future pattern of church government, little was said positively about worship, nothing was said about endowment. The reformers had already prepared at least part of a programme for the reform of administration and endowment, in the shape of a 'Book of Reformation', but this seems to have been ignored. The interest of the dominant faction, headed by nobles whose families were already, in one guise or another, well entrenched in church property, was the maintenance of the status quo in endowment. This fact helped to produce inactivity in matters relating to church government as well. Many of the bishops were closely related to the leading noble families, and there could be no question of depriving them and replacing them by protestants. Persuasion, indeed, could be tried, and was tried, though with imperfect success, for no more than four bishops definitely committed themselves to the reformed Church, and only three took it into their hands to organize the reformed Church in their dioceses. Generally throughout the country there was as yet no reformed organization at any level above the parish, and the system, if there was one, was little more than what would now be called congregational.

Militant opposition to the ecclesiastical changes had been almost non-existent, but the victorious Protestants had to safeguard themselves against a counter-offensive from France, which would rally the very considerable amount of latent sympathy with the Roman cause. They had also to take into account the possibility that Mary would remain in France, a possibility perhaps now stronger than ever. For a dozen years or more, as long almost as she could remember, her life and prospects had been shaped by her position in France, first as intended bride of the Dauphin, then as Dauphiness, and finally, since July 1559, as Queen of France. Of her eighteen years, she had spent more than two-thirds in France, and the Scotland of her childhood can have meant little to her. Therefore, the Scottish leaders, besides sending a representative to ask for a formal ratification of the Treaty of Edinburgh, pressed for an agreement with England which would have produced an effective alliance, and perhaps a union, of the two countries. The recent revolution had been, besides much else, a triumph for the Hamiltons. Châtelherault and his son Young Arran were at the head of the provisional government and this position, if not the throne itself, might continue to be theirs should Mary perhaps decide not to try to re-establish control over a country which had decisively rejected French policies. This greatly strengthened the case for a marriage between Young Arran and the Queen of England, and the proposal gained very wide support among the Scots, even from some who had not been enthusiastic about the recent revolution. An impressive embassy went off in October 1560 to ask for a permanent alliance with England and to propose the marriage of Arran and Elizabeth.

The whole situation, both of the reforming party in Scotland and of Anglo-Scottish relations, was changed when, on 5 December 1560, Mary's husband died. Knox remarked that 'the King's death made great alteration in France, England, and Scotland'. In France, the new King was Charles IX, a boy of ten, and the Guise family, which had been in the ascendant when their kinswoman, Mary, was Queen Consort, lost ground to the Queen Mother, Catherine de' Medici. Catherine had had to take second place to her husband's mistress in his lifetime and to Mary during the brief reign of Francis, but had nevertheless been of more account under Francis, and Mary and she had seen much of each other. Although Catherine had at one time been proposed as a bride for Mary's father, James V, she lacked the royal birth appropriate to a wife of a King of France, and when she married the future Henry II he was not heir apparent, for his elder brother was still alive. Mary's alleged remark that Catherine was only 'the daughter of a merchant' is not well authenticated, but there may have been some tension and jealousy. Catherine, an older and personally unattractive woman, can hardly have applauded Mary's charms, and there may also have been a competitive element in their affection for Francis. Then, while Catherine must have appreciated the way in which Mary contributed to the happiness of Francis while he lived, she had less use for her after his death. It was Catherine who was now, with the death of Francis, the effective ruler of France. Mary, on the other hand, was now nothing more in France than a widowed queen, and it therefore seemed likely that she would prefer to return to Scotland as Queen Regnant.

In France, then, there was an 'alteration', but its ultimate effects for Mary and for Scotland were as yet imponderable. The 'alteration' in England was that Queen Elizabeth rejected the suit of the Earl of Arran three days after the death of Francis; apparently she had not yet received the news of the event, but he had been dangerously ill for weeks and, if she had good reason to know that his death was certainly predicted, she may have calculated that Mary would return to Scotland, where Arran would be a suitable husband who would guide her into the ways of the Reformation. In Scotland Knox himself contributed to an 'alteration': as soon as he had assurance privately that the illness of Francis was mortal he set out to confer with Châtelherault, and they advised Young Arran to reopen communication with his old sweetheart, Mary. This, it may be guessed, Arran was nothing loth to do, for did he not have a ring as a pledge from their childhood days in France? It has to be recalled that there had been considerable support for an Arran-Mary match in 1544–6. Since then the children had been taken to France within weeks of each other in 1548 and, although there were other plans at a political level for the marriage of each of them, there was a kind of boy and girl affair, as a result of which Arran was led to understand that if the arrangements for Mary's marriage to the Dauphin came adrift he could expect consideration as a suitor. At this stage, in December 1560, he was 'not altogether without hope that the Queen of Scotland bore him some favour', so he wrote to Mary and sent her the ring, which she 'knew well enough'. Châtelherault saw in the marriage of Mary and Arran the assured future for his house which he had been seeking at every opportunity since Mary's birth, and Knox – for once in agreement with Elizabeth – saw in the marriage of Mary to Arran security for the reforming cause in Scotland. Finally, while Mary's prospects in France had been extinguished by the death of Francis, her prospects in England were at least deferred by the obvious acquiescence of most Englishmen in the rule of Elizabeth.

But supposing the Queen were to return determined to overthrow the Reformation? She would not now bring French help, at least on any scale, but she could rally the anti-Protestant and conservative elements. Faced with this threat, the reforming party could no longer allow the indeterminate situation of their church to continue. A convention of the nobility was summoned for January, but even earlier, on 20 December, a convention of representatives of some of the reformed congregations met and resumed work on the Book of Reformation. Probably its revision and expansion was entrusted to committees, whose work was approved when the ecclesiastical convention reassembled on 15 January. The programme for polity and endowment was then presented to the secular convention, which looked askance at the sweeping claims the reformers made to ecclesiastical property, and when a considerable number of nobles and lairds approved the Book on 27 January they did so only with the proviso that all holders of ecclesiastical offices who supported the Reformation should continue to enjoy their revenues for their lifetimes but should make some contribution to the support of ministers.

The approval of the 'Book of Discipline', as it had now become, though disappointing on the financial side, did provide machinery for setting up a regional organization for the Church. The programme was for ten superintendents or reformed bishops, each responsible for the oversight of his diocese but possessing none of the sacramental functions of an episcopate. In March and April 1561 the first superintendents were nominated by the council to Lothian and Fife, and three others were appointed later. There was no need for superintendents where the bishops were actively furthering the Reformation, and some care seems to have been taken not to make an appointment in any diocese where there was still some hope that the bishop would be won over. Supreme authority over the reformed Church was evidently intended to rest with the privy council, in whose name the superintendents acted. The Book of Discipline had done no more than refer in wonderfully vague terms to a 'Council of the Church', and it is far from clear whether either this proposed council or the conventions of representatives of congregations which met in December 1560 and May 1561 can really be regarded as the earliest of the 'general assemblies' which were to direct church affairs after Mary's return.

3 The Politic Ruler

The return to Scotland in 1561 was the first occasion on which Mary's own wishes helped to shape her future. Her departure for France in 1548, her marriage to Francis, had been determined for her by others, but now, at the age of eighteen, she had the capacity to choose for herself. It is not hard to discern the considerations which may have weighed with her. The very bases of her life had been shattered. Not only had she lost the boy-husband from whom she had never been long apart since they had first met when she was six, but, a year before, her dear friend and sister-in-law, the Princess Elizabeth, had left France to be married to Philip of Spain, and, six months before, her mother had died. That Mary should remain in France as an unmarried widow, overshadowed by Catherine de' Medici and ultimately by Catherine's sons, was not to be thought of. It is true that Mary could have married the brother and successor of Francis, Charles IX, and thus, after a minority dominated by Catherine, have regained her position, but such a match can hardly have been attractive on personal grounds. On the other hand, a match with a French nobleman or with some minor continental royalty was not consonant with Mary's dignity. Scotland now offered her better prospects, if only as a step to England, on which her heart was set.

But if Mary was this time going to make the decision for herself, there were plenty of others ready to make a decision for her. As ever, she was a figure in European, not only in Scottish, politics. She was the most desirable match on the Continent, and John Knox had not been alone in at once looking for a successor to Francis. The King was hardly dead when other pos-

sible bridegrooms were put forward in addition to Charles IX.
One of them was Mary's cousin, Lord Darnley, whom she
ultimately did marry and who had been thought of as a possible
bridegroom for her almost since his birth three years after her
own. The King of Navarre thought of divorcing his wife to
marry Mary. Frederick of Denmark and Erik of Sweden transferred their suits from Elizabeth to her. Others in the field were
the Duke of Finland (brother of the Swedish King) and two sons
of the Emperor. For a time the most likely candidate seemed to
be Don Carlos, son of Philip II of Spain. This match must have
tempted Mary's ambitions, for it offered a throne at least the
equal of that of France, it offered the prospect of Spanish assistance to make good her claim to England, and, at the personal
level, it would reunite her to Elizabeth, her sister-in-law. Carlos
was nearly as old as Francis had been, and had not yet shown
the hopeless imbecility which was to end his career. However,
there were difficulties. King Philip had no desire at this juncture
to offend Elizabeth of England, which a match between his son
and her intended supplanter would have done; and Catherine
de' Medici, who was the effective ruler of France, calculated
that such a brilliant marriage for Mary would raise the prestige
of the Guise family once more and threaten the position of her
daughter Elizabeth, who, if Don Carlos died, might be the mother
of a future King of Spain. When enthusiasm for the Spanish
match cooled, the attractions of Scotland, where Mary might be
able to strengthen her position by being a Queen Regnant, without necessarily sacrificing her prospects in the European marriage market, grew in proportion.

What manner of woman was she who decided to return to
Scotland as its Queen, and how far had her character and outlook been shaped by the thirteen years she had spent in
France? Mary has always had a great reputation as a charmer,
but it is not easy to form a clear impression of the precise nature
of her attractions. There is little in her portraits to suggest over-
powering beauty and – although one would have expected her
portraits to be flattering – it has been suggested that they cannot
do her justice, for they assuredly do not show a woman who

would captivate by her appearance. It should be said that we
have no portraits professing to show her when she was probably
at her best, for there is none depicting her as she was from the
time she left France until after she had begun her English captivity – that is, we have no picture of Mary between the ages of
nineteen and twenty-five or indeed a few years later. We do
have portraits showing her as a girl and in her early widowhood
after the death of Francis, the best of them being the *deuil blanc*
portrait by Clouet, showing her in mourning for her first husband. The most familiar, because most frequently reproduced,
portraits are from Mary's later years, when she was shaping as
the Roman Catholic martyr, and seem to originate with a rather
indifferent miniature done at Sheffield by Nicholas Hilliard in
1577 or 1578. The 'Sheffield portrait' was frequently copied
for circulation among Mary's co-religionists on the Continent
both before and after her death. The material point is that the
Mary of the portraits is either immature or worn by captivity.

Yet if the portraits do not impress, there is little in authentic
descriptions which indicate that they are gravely at fault. It
was only poets who suggested that Mary was a ravishing beauty.
Sir James Melville called her 'very lovesome', the people of
Edinburgh hailed her 'sweet face', and John Knox's adjective –
though he would not exaggerate her charms – was 'pleasing'.
Mary's grandmother, speaking of her childhood appearance, had
reservations: although her complexion was fine and clear –
smallpox left her skin unmarked – and the lower part of her
face pretty, the eyes were small and deep-set and the face rather
long. The portraits on the whole bear this out, for her nose does
seem long, her forehead rather high, and it is hard to believe
that the hint of a cast in the eye was the invention of an artist.
(It seems that Bothwell, her third husband, had lost an eye, and
it is surprising that their marriage has not recalled the 'one-
eyed drummer who loved the cock-eyed cook'.)

Her features aside, there were other characteristics which
made up the woman the Scots knew between 1561 and 1567.
Mary had begun to show signs of recurrent illness in early
adolescence, and in 1559 she was several times reported to be

IV Francis II, Mary's first husband – drawing by Clouet

III Mary aged sixteen – drawing by Clouet

VI   The James V Tower at Holyrood

V   The Château of Chenonceaux

very ill. What was obviously a gastric trouble and for years was apt to be brought on by any crisis, was probably psychosomatic in origin. During her illnesses she may often have looked worse than she was, with her pale and clear complexion. It is true that she often displayed remarkable powers of endurance, but this may have lain in nervous, rather than physical, strength, and it is difficult to avoid the conclusion that she showed a certain physical fragility which may have enhanced her attractions. She was very tall – almost six feet – and, although she does not seem to have inherited the stateliness which accompanied her mother's comparable stature, she had a conspicuously graceful carriage. She also had a pleasant voice. But one suspects that it was above all her charm of manner which made her attractive and that her personality, warm, lively, and vivacious, shaped the expression of eyes and mouth in a way that no portrait could convey. Not the least of her charms was a natural kindness – which in a Queen was condescension, though in Mary it was so graciously and naturally given that neither she nor her subjects thought of it as condescension. It was this characteristic which led to an occasional familiarity with servants and other inferiors which some thought indiscreet, but it caused her to stand well with her subjects throughout her realm as well as with her courtiers and advisers. Sir James Melville, who relates so much about the courts of Mary and Elizabeth, recounts how after a serious discussion with her one evening at Stirling, 'the supper being ended, Her Majesty took me by the hand and went down through the park of Stirling, and came up through the town, ever reasoning with me upon these purposes.' We shall see later how profound an impression Mary made on the Englishmen whom she met when she fled from Scotland in 1568 and who praised the 'eloquent tongue', 'stout courage and liberal heart', and 'ready wit' of this 'puissant lady'.

The life of the French court in which Mary grew up had been shaped to some extent by Francis I, an ambitious warrior but also a patron of scholars, poets, painters, and sculptors and the builder of Fontainebleau, Blois, and Chambord. But Francis died in 1547, and the France Mary knew for thirteen years was that of his son, Henry II. She was accustomed to life on the most lavish scale, with an enormous household and a vast wardrobe, for under Henry II the splendour and extravagance of the court, as well as the patronage of the arts, continued. But Henry was not notable for either force of character or intellectual ability. Influence over him lay with his mistress, Diane de Poitiers, and effective power was something to be competed for by the leading noble families, though their rivalry was to some extent kept in check by the mere existence of an adult king. It was after Henry's death that the reigns of his young sons were to give greater opportunities to the nobles.

Of one of the leading families, that of Guise, Queen Mary was a member through her mother, and her life in France is to be seen in a Guise context. Claude, Duke of Guise, Mary's grandfather, died in 1550, and it was her six uncles who were in the ascendancy in France in the later years of Henry II – Francis, Duke of Guise, Charles, Cardinal of Lorraine, Claude, Duke of Aumale, Louis, Cardinal of Guise, René, Marquis of Elboeuf, and Francis, Grand Prior of the Order of St John. Though not in the succession to the ruling French house of Valois, the Guise family could claim descent from Charlemagne, but they owed as much to their ability and personality as to their lineage. It was the Duke of Guise who distinguished himself by holding Metz against the Emperor in a famous siege in 1552–3 and who led the army which captured Calais from the English in January 1558; and three months after that victory his niece, Mary Stewart, married the eldest son of Henry II. This seemed to assure the future of the house of Guise in the contest for power in France. But they had rivals in the house of Bourbon, which stood next in the succession after the reigning family of Valois, and that of Montmorency, which was led by the Constable of France until his death in 1567.

The family rivalries were intensified by religious differences. Protestantism had existed in some strength even in Francis I's reign, but more recently the situation had been shaped largely by the proximity of Calvin's Geneva, a kind of power-house of revolt against the institutions and the dogmas of the Catholic

Church and the breeding-place for dozens of pastors who minis-
tered to French congregations. Calvinism won many recruits in
France among the bourgeousie and the legal profession and also,
as time passed, among the nobility and gentry. Before Mary left
France in 1561, the Huguenots were holding public services in
many places, they were taking over parish churches and
evidently had in all more than 2,000 congregations, with, it was
claimed, 300,000 members. In their great stronghold of Orleans
some 5,000 to 6,000 persons were attending Protestant Communion services. The first national synod of the reformed
Church was held in May 1559, and, although it was a small and
clandestine affair, it led to the adoption of a formal organization
to bind the congregations together.

Of the three leading families, that of Bourbon, headed by the
vacillating Antoine, King of Navarre, and his more resolute
younger brother, Louis, Prince of Condé, adopted the Huguenot
cause; and, while the Constable Montmorency remained on the
conservative side, his three nephews were Huguenots, and one of
them was Gaspard de Coligny, the Admiral of France. The Guise
family, on the other hand, stood by the Church. At a later stage
they were to become renowned for their bigoted ruthlessness
in defending orthodoxy, but as yet they were not all wholly
intransigent. It has to be remembered that, besides Protestantism, there was in France a good deal of non-Roman Catholicism, or Gallicanism. One of Mary's uncles, the Cardinal of Lorraine, was in favour of Communion in both kinds and the autho-
rization of the Liturgy in the vernacular; it was even said that he
commended the English Prayer Book to his niece. There were,
however, many executions of Huguenots during the Guise
ascendancy, and it was inevitable that the Guises should be a
target for Huguenot attacks. In March 1560 there was a conspiracy, designed as a palace revolution with the object of dis-
placing the Guises from their position about the King and of
killing them if they resisted. The execution of the plot was entrusted to Godfrey de la Renaudie, while Condé, the real leader,
was to arrive after it had been carried out. The conspirators
were frustrated, and the Guises took a bloody vengeance in the

'massacre of Amboise'. The devious Condé was able to deny complicity.

When Catherine de' Medici became the real ruler of France after the death of Francis II, her antagonism to the Guises would of itself have made her inclined to a moderate policy in religion, but she was also by temperament disposed to conciliation. In September 1561 there was held, on her initiative, the Colloquy of Poissy, at which an attempt was made to reconcile Catholics and Huguenots, and for a time Catherine seemed in a fair way to gaining papal consent to certain concessions which Protestants demanded. The Colloquy was a failure, but the fact that it had been held encouraged the Huguenots. In January 1562 the government conceded to the Huguenots a measure of toleration or licensed co-existence as the only practicable solution of the problem, and Catherine even prevailed on the Pope to give a degree of approval to this. The Guise faction were so hostile to Catherine's policy that they now left the court, and in the next year the Duke of Guise was murdered by a Huguenot. Wars, feuds, and conspiracies continued.

The France which Mary Stewart left in August 1561 was assuredly no model of stability. There is no reason to believe that she had taken a keen interest in current affairs, still less played a part in them, but there were certain things of which she must have become aware. One lesson she had learned was the meaning of a contest for power among great families, another was the impact of the Reformation. She had seen bigotry on both sides, but she had also seen efforts at conciliation. She had seen how religion and politics were involved in the strife of faction. While she was strictly drilled in religious observance, and the round of services of the Catholic Church must have seemed an indispensable part of life, she knew many who thought differently and others who were prepared to compromise. She was familiar with a prelate – the Cardinal of Lorraine – who was also a dynastic statesman; she was acquainted with the subtlety of a politician like Condé. She had seen battle, murder, and sudden death.

Mary received instruction in the accomplishments appropriate to a princess of the time. She learned Italian and Spanish, she understood Latin well enough though she was less proficient at speaking it, and she may have known some Greek, for there were Greek books in her library as well as books in the other tongues she knew, with French predominating and a preponderance of poetry and history. She was taught drawing and dancing and she played on the lute as well as on the virginals – though on the latter only 'reasonably well for a queen', according to Sir James Melville. She was certainly very fond of music : not only did she think it an essential part of the secular life of her court, but she was eager to have it at Mass as often as possible. While she was not allowed to forget the Scots language which had been her tongue in infancy, there is no evidence that her education included systematic instruction in the affairs of a country in which, until the death of Francis, she cannot have expected to live again. But her residence in France was no bad apprenticeship. Mary's inexperience when she left France in her nineteenth year, her innocence of the ways of self-seeking and brutal men, can be exaggerated.

Mary's decision to return to Scotland was only the first of the decisions she had to make : the country was not so much at peace as in a state of armistice, under a provisional government of dubious legality, and Mary had to make up her mind which party, which individuals, which interest, she would support and rely on. The reforming faction, besides organizing its Church and preparing for a situation in which it might have to survive under an unsympathetic ruler, nevertheless took steps to ensure that Mary was at least in no doubt about the conditions under which they would have her reign should she return to Scotland. Immediately after the parliament of August 1560 they sent the enthusiastic Protestant James Sandilands, Preceptor of the House of the Knights of St John at Torphichen – a position which had for long provided only the thinnest of disguises for a layman who was commonly known as 'Lord St John' – to France to crave Mary's ratification of the new legislation. He was back in Scotland in December, after a mission which had proved fruitless. But, when, after the death of Francis, the reformers came to put their case afresh before Mary, they found that they were not of one mind. We hear much from Knox about a thorough-going and unyielding attitude which would not have acquiesced in the celebration of Mass under any conditions, but it is not clear how many of the other preachers supported the extremist; among laymen, Young Arran evidently adopted this line, though there were others who were not disposed either to advance the house of Hamilton or coerce the Queen, and even Arran's own family was not united, for Archbishop John Hamilton took up an equivocal position.

In the end, it was neither Knox nor Arran who went to France as the spokesman of the reformers, but the Lord James Stewart, who showed before he went that he regarded the policy of the extremists as impracticable:

He was plainly premonished [wrote Knox] that if ever he con-descended that she should have Mass publicly or privately within the realm of Scotland, then he betrayed the cause of God. . . . That she should have Mass publicly, he affirmed he should never consent; but to have it secretly in her chamber, who could stop her?

Lord James left Scotland on 18 March and was back in Edin-burgh on 29 May, to report to a convention of estates. Although the presumption is that he had reached an understanding with Mary, at least at a personal level, it is not known what official news he brought; but the convention declined to renew the old alliance with France and agreed, at the instance of the reformed Church, to proceedings against 'idolatry'. The likelihood is that Lord James had indicated that Mary could count on the obedience of her subjects provided that she did not come as a spearhead of a renewed French attempt to dominate Scotland and did not take positive action to reverse the ecclesiastical revolution; but it was plain that Mary could expect only quali-fied, or at least conditional, support from the provisional govern-ment. Yet Lord James's proposition cannot have been unattrac-tive in contrast to the other options. The extreme Protestants would allow Mary no freedom of action, and to surrender to them was distasteful, probably because she had a genuine enough preference for the Mass, but possibly also because she did not want to alienate either the papalist powers of the Continent or the Roman Catholics of England. Besides, she had good reason for refusing to be dragooned into a marriage with Young Arran. Whatever charms he may have had in her girlish eyes in France, he was by now showing signs of the mental breakdown which he suffered within a matter of months, and even if he had still been personally attractive he was a poor alternative to some of her other suitors.

The Scottish Roman Catholics, on their side, had little to offer Mary, for it is not at all clear if there really was such a thing as a Roman Catholic party in Scotland. The critics or opponents of the Reformation were still ineffective and demoralized, and the prospect of Mary's return seems to have done little to rouse them. The only out-and-out papalist among the bishops had left for France in 1560, never to return, and his example hardly induced optimism. None of the other bishops had been prepared to make an unqualified stand against the legislation of 1560, and laymen were so dismayed by their apparent pusillanimity that only three or four peers voted against the reformers' programme. The three or four did not include the Earl of Huntly, the greatest magnate of the north-east, which was potentially the rallying ground for the conservatives, for he had sided with the insurgents in the early months of 1560. It is true that, while Huntly evidently had no enthusiasm for Rome, he would almost certainly have supported Mary had she chosen to head a reaction; but, with his record, it was impossible to trust any offers he may now have made. It is true, of course, that the reforming Church was as yet a struggling infant, hardly organized outside certain limited areas, and there was an enormous amount of latent sympathy and inarticulate preference for the old ways, but no one could say how far these sentiments would or would not respond to leadership. It would have been folly for Mary – a woman quite unknown to all but a handful of her Scottish subjects – to set herself up as the head of what was little better than a hypothetical movement, especially at a time when she could not expect effective support from France in pursuing a papalist policy.

While superficially there were resemblances between the French situation and the Scottish, it is creditable to Mary's intelligence that she grasped both that the Scottish Protestants had gained a degree of success which had so far eluded the Huguenots and that the Roman Catholics were temporarily demoralized in Scotland in a way they never were in France. There was much to be gained, and little to be lost, by adopting a relatively noncommittal policy, which was that advocated by Lord James. While there is no question of the sincerity of his attachment to the reformed Church, he was too much the politician to follow the example of Arran and Knox. In his moderate policy he had the support of the subtle Secretary of State, William Maitland of Lethington, sometimes known as 'Mitchell Wylie', a Scoticization of Machiavelli. Their concept of recognition of the reformed Church while the Queen had her own Mass chimed in with Mary's own preferences and left the door open for appeals to continental and English Roman Catholics. On the political side, an understanding with Elizabeth (though Mary may have had limited enthusiasm for it) had much to commend it, even if only as an interim policy.

Although, as events were to show, Lord James was a skilful advocate of his own case, competing views were being presented to the Queen by his rivals or critics. There was the bearer of Arran's ring; there was the ecclesiastical lawyer John Lesley, urging her (according to his own account) to make for Aberdeenshire and join forces with Huntly; there was the Earl of Bothwell, whose combination of firm Protestantism with detestation of England and loyalty to Mary's late mother illustrated the complexities of the Scottish scene. Mary was at the same time a target for the applications of those who came from Scotland to accompany her home or to put before her either their personal grievances or their ambitions: there was, for example, Adam Bothwell, Bishop of Orkney, complaining (with just cause) that laymen were making such inroads on his revenues that he could not make ends meet on the pittance left to him;

there were former servants of her mother, like Francisco de Busso, who expected rewards; there were office-seekers, for appointments had to be made to such offices as Comptroller, General of the Mint, and Lyon King of Arms. In dealing with these applications by letters issued in France, Mary was initiated into Scottish administration. Pestered also by English envoys urging her to ratify the Treaty of Edinburgh, and bombarded simultaneously by the suits of a range of possible husbands, it is no wonder that, although she tried to keep the suppliants at bay by making a leisured progress through France to Lorraine, she had at this stage one of those illnesses which attacked her in times of stress.

While it can hardly be doubted that the choice Mary made before she left France was her own, there is no reason to think that it was displeasing to her French friends. The advice she received from them was, so it was said, 'to serve the time, to accommodate herself discreetly and gently to her own subjects . . . and, in effect, to repose most upon those of the reformed religion'. The task of ruling Scotland had, after all, been in the hands of her French mother until a year before. Not only did her Guise kinsfolk give her a good send-off, but three of her uncles – the Dukes of Elboeuf and Aumale and the Grand Prior – accompanied her to Scotland.

Elizabeth showed no readiness to give Mary a safe-conduct through England – the first of many occasions when she shrank from the opportunity of meeting her cousin – and this meant preparations for a journey by sea. The English Queen can hardly have been eager to admit to her realm a rival who had not laid aside a claim to her crown, and she may have feared the renewal of French influence in Scotland. But could she prevent Mary's return, and if so, how? She did send ships to sea, but it has been suggested that the object was not to intercept Mary but possibly to prevent her from landing among the Roman Catholics of northern England, possibly to compel her to take the west-coast route, which would have brought her to the Firth of Clyde and Dumbarton, where Arran and the Hamiltons were waiting for her. There is much to support this latter suggestion, but had Elizabeth wanted to shepherd Mary in any direction the simplest way would surely have been to grant her a safe-conduct through England under surveillance and with an honourable escort who could see to it that she fell into the hands of Elizabeth's Scottish friends.

The English Queen may indeed have made this calculation, for a safe-conduct was ultimately sent, but it reached France only after Mary had left. The party sailed from Calais on 14 August and the oarsmen of her galleys made a swift passage through timely fogs to reach Leith on 19 August, a week before they were expected. Even so, English ships saluted Mary's own flotilla and allowed it to proceed. The rest of the fleet was examined for pirates, but the only loss was of the ship containing Mary's stable, which put in at Tynemouth and was detained there for a month because it lacked a passport. It would seem that although an English fleet was thus hovering around, Elizabeth had characteristically given it no adequate instructions for action, and, of course, the arrest of Mary would have been so embarrassing to Elizabeth as to be unthinkable.

There is no mistaking the character of the policy which Mary and her advisers at once adopted. The privy council which was constituted on her return contained no prelates and its most conservative member was the somewhat equivocal Huntly. Mary insisted that Mass should be said at court for herself and her French entourage, but, while this perhaps did something to make the old rite fashionable, there is no indication that it was deliberately intended as an instrument to proselytize. Concurrently, the Queen forbade by proclamation 'any alteration or innovation of the state of religion . . . which Her Majesty found public and universally standing at Her Majesty's arrival in this her realm'. It may not have escaped notice that a somewhat similar proclamation had been issued by Elizabeth on her accession and it could be read as a sign that there was to be at least no hasty counter-revolution. Although Mary always refused to ratify the Acts of August 1560, including the one condemning the Mass, her reason must have been the doubtful legality of the parliament which had passed them rather than any objection to their substance, for her administration was conducted very much as if these Acts had the force of law. She several times reissued her initial proclamation to reassure the Protestants, and, although her own chaplains were protected, other priests, including Archbishop Hamilton, were prosecuted and imprisoned for saying Mass in violation of the Queen's proclamation.

Somewhat similarly, although Mary would not consent to a sweeping dispossession of the clergy and other holders of church property, and her return gave an opportunity to the prelates to 'grip again to that which most unjustly they called their own', she agreed in February 1562 to a scheme whereby one-third of the revenues of most benefices was collected by crown officials and used partly to augment her own revenues and partly to pay stipends to the clergy of the reformed Church. The remaining two-thirds remained with the existing possessors, and Knox characterized the arrangement as 'two-thirds freely given to the devil and the third divided between God and the devil'. In the first year that the scheme operated, out of £53,000 available for distribution, the Crown received less than a quarter, the reformed Church a half, and there was an unexpended balance of £5,000. As the crown revenues in 1560 had been only about £40,000, and as the Treasurer had a deficit which by 1564 was to amount to £33,000, the government yielded to temptation. That money should be going a-begging was a novelty for the impecunious Scottish monarchy, and means were soon found to swallow up the balance. From the outset the cost of the Queen's bodyguard was met from the thirds, and as time passed they were drawn on for household outlays, the Queen's travelling expenses, the transport of musical instruments from France, and payments to musicians.

The fact that Mary was depending on church revenues for such purposes – not to mention for £50 given to her to 'play at the cards' – gave her something of a vested interest in the Reformation. Nor was this vested interest confined to the ability to raid the thirds. The fact was that, in pursuance of a trend discernible even before the death of James V, the Crown now assumed papal, and more than papal, powers over the disposition of offices in the Church and the revenues attached to them, and made appointments to bishoprics, abbeys, and lesser benefices. This situation enabled Mary, like her wiser predecessors, to carry on her government without much recourse to taxation, and the only tax raised in her personal reign was one of £40,000 for her son's baptism in 1566. All this made it evident that a simple reversal of the decision of 1560 was out of the question. Further recognition of the status of the reformed Church came in 1563, with a statute which gave its clergy the right to enjoy the manses and glebes attached to parish churches, and in the same year there were wholesale prosecutions of Mass-mongers.

It was quite consonant with these proceedings that Mary gave little encouragement to the Jesuit de Gouda, who came to Scotland as a papal representative in 1562, and that she did not arrange for Scottish representation at the last session of the Council of Trent. Nor had she any scruples about attending at least one baptism conducted according to Protestant rites, and, as she attended the festivities connected with the weddings of Protestant half-brothers and other kinsfolk, she may well have been present at the religious ceremonies also. On the other hand, apart from occasionally intervening to protect an individual Roman Catholic from harsh treatment, she did little for those commonly regarded as her co-religionists. From time to time she reassured the Pope with fair words, even to the extent of declaring that she was doing her best to make a number of prelates go to Trent; as she could have nominated two Scottish bishops who were already on the Continent – Beaton of Glasgow and Chisholm of Dunblane – this looks like a direct lie. Anyone could see how hard it was to reconcile her words with her actions, which were disappointing to zealous Roman Catholics, as she herself was well aware, for in January 1563 she asked the Cardinal of Lorraine to make excuses for her if she had failed in her duty towards religion.

Those who see Mary as at heart an enthusiastic Roman Catholic rather than an opportunist politician are apt to single out her reassurances to the Pope as more sincere and as more indicative of her real intent than her reassurances to the Protestants and even than the policy she was putting into practice. Perhaps it is here that there has been the principal divergence in judgments on her. However, the presentation of Mary, at this stage in her career, as a devotee of Rome, simply will not do. Her troubles in Scotland were not to arise from her pursuance of a papalist policy: how they did arise will emerge later, but it is worth remembering that her supposed fidelity to Rome had nothing to do with her downfall and that when, on the most dismal day of her life, she was insulted by the women of her capital, it was not 'Burn the papist' that they shouted, but 'Burn the whore'.

From the outset, Mary's tolerant and perhaps equivocal policy found some influential support. On the first Sunday after her return, when the mob would have lynched the priest who said her Mass, the doors were guarded (ostensibly, so Knox said, to prevent Scots from entering) by three of her half-brothers, Lords James, Robert, and John, all of them members of the reformed Church. It is true that others thought differently. The Earl of Arran made a formal protest against the terms of Mary's initial proclamation, in so far as it protected her French servants in their 'idolatry', and he refused to come to court as long as Mass was said there. The town council of Edinburgh issued a proclamation classing Mass-mongers with whoremongers, and when the Queen went on progress her Mass caused local disturbances.

The chief irreconcilable was John Knox, who lost no time in denouncing the Queen's Mass and remarked sourly that at the palace there was 'some enchantment whereby men are bewitched'. He had several interviews with the Queen in which, according to his own account – and no other has come down to us – he took a strong, even hectoring, line. His readiness to confront this woman is in sharp contrast to his earlier refusal to face what the administrations of Mary of Guise and Mary Tudor could do, and the explanation is to be found not only in the strength now of his own position but in his knowledge of Mary Stewart's tolerance. Although, in a sermon and in one of his

interviews, he denounced Mary's marriage plans, it was characteristic of her régime, and characteristic of the Scotland of that
period, that no proceedings were taken against him, whereas
poor John Stubbs, who similarly denounced Queen Elizabeth's
projected marriage with a French prince, had his right hand cut
off. Knox's views were coloured not only by his sufferings in the
galleys, where a constant dread of the lash possibly induced that
physical fear by which he was to be persistently afflicted, but
also by his terror when Edward VI was succeeded by Mary
Tudor in England, his defeat by more traditionally-minded
Englishmen at Frankfort, and his sojourn at Geneva.

But no other Scots had had these experiences, and no more
than two or three others had come directly under Calvin's influence. There were more who had come under Lutheran or
Anglican influence and who differed from Knox in their views
on church affairs as well as in their attitude to the Queen. Not
many shared Knox's view that all Mary's concessions to his
party sprang from dissimulation, and the breach between him
and the moderates became evident in 1563, when Lord James
and he ceased to be on speaking terms. Although, as minister of
the capital, Knox had a position of unique influence, his views
were not typical; the trouble was that, although he did not speak
for all, he never – at least according to his own account – had
any hesitation in speaking. He found he was getting less and
less support, and the 'enchantment whereby men are bewitched'
was, admittedly, one reason. It is true that it did not take long
for Mary's charm to have its effect on those who met her, and
her personality reinforced the appeal of the undoubted wisdom
of her policy. An adult sovereign had not held court at Holyrood since 1542, and this sovereign was a young woman with a
gifted personality.

If Mary's policy stirred up only a limited, and dwindling,
amount of Protestant opposition, it did nothing, on the other
side, to encourage, far less rally, the dispirited Roman Catholics. Just as extreme Protestants, like Knox and Arran, disapproved of Mary's moderation, so a conservative like Huntly
may have disapproved of concessions to the reformed Church.

Yet when Huntly rose in rebellion in 1562 he found his challenge was taken up by the Queen. Religion was not, indeed, the issue on which he resorted to arms. One reason was that he had a personal feud with Lord James as well as a disagreement with him on policy: Huntly had been administering the earldoms of Mar and Moray, which had been vacant, but gifts of them in favour of Lord James were drawn up at the beginning of 1562. It was also true that Sir John Gordon, Huntly's third son, had designs on the Queen and it was even believed that he contemplated seizing her person. Sir John, as it happened, had assaulted Lord Ogilvie and had acquired lands which should have been inherited by another Ogilvie, and when Mary set out on a northern progress in August 1562 she intended to bring him to book. When she reached Inverness, she found the castle barred against her on the orders of Lord Gordon, Huntly's heir, and the captain of the castle was executed. Huntly himself was summoned to appear before the privy council, but refused to obey and marched on Aberdeen after Mary had returned to that town. He was defeated at Corrichie (28 October) and died suddenly after his capture. He was condemned posthumously for treason, and his estates were forfeited to the Crown; Sir John Gordon was executed, and Lord Gordon and the Earl of Sutherland (Huntly's cousin) were condemned to death but pardoned. The army which defeated Huntly was led by the new Earl of Moray. Although Knox alleged that Mary was displeased by Huntly's overthrow, and this may have been true in one sense, yet the affair showed clearly enough that a preference for Rome (if Huntly had such a preference) was not regarded as an excuse for rebellion. Half a year after Corrichie, Mary held her first parliament, at which Huntly and Sutherland forfeited their estates and which passed legislation suggesting that she had reached an accommodation with the reformed Church. It was perhaps the apogee of her reign; there hardly seemed a cloud in the sky.

Mary's policy in all her doings was such as to win support from fairminded men and from all whose minds were not closed to the consideration of her merits. It is true that her actions,

especially in permitting Protestantism for her subjects but in-
sisting on Catholicism for herself, suggest opportunism and
self-interest: she would be all things to all men and commend
herself to the dominant Protestants in Scotland and England
without alienating the Roman Catholic minority there or the
Roman Catholic powers on the Continent. Cecil's comment in
1562 that Mary was 'no more devout towards Rome than for
the contentation of her uncles' ignores the liberal views of the
Cardinal of Lorraine but shows at least that the subtle English
Secretary appreciated Mary's adaptability. Others could take
a more generous view, and reflect that she had done much to
fulfil the hopes expressed on her arrival in 1561:

> Found on the first four virtues cardinal,
> On wisdom, justice, force and temperance . . . .
> Cause staunch all strife and stable thy estates
> In constance, concord, charity and love.

Mary was in fact successful in bringing about a unity among the
Scottish magnates which had hardly been paralleled since the
days of her grandfather James IV.

There is no doubt, either, about her personal popularity among
her subjects. She behaved as people thought a queen should. She
had, as she explained to Knox, been brought up in 'joyousity'
in France, and few of her subjects – although she complained,
it was said, of their 'gravity' – thought there was anything
indecorous about her recreations. Indoors she had a craze for
embroidery which persisted throughout her life, she was fond
of masques, music, cards, dice, and dancing (which even Knox
did not 'utterly condemn'). Some 'gravity' was not ruled out,
because after dinner she would read Livy with George Buchanan,
a sixty-year-old scholar of distinction who had spent much
time in France and Portugal and, though he was a member of the
reformed Church, represented cosmopolitan humanism. Out
of doors she enjoyed archery, hunting, hawking, and golf. She
loved to wear male costume and go through the streets incog-
nito; at a banquet to the French ambassador she and her Maries
appeared dressed as men, and when she took the field with her

soldiers she dressed as a man. A six-footer like her mother, she could 'play the man', and her stature was to her advantage when she was thus disguised, unlike her descendant, Bonnie Prince Charlie, who made such a poor show when he was disguised as 'Betty Burke'. Mary's tall, athletic figure could be seen to advantage as she made her frequent progresses among her people. Each year from to 1562 to 1566 she was in Fife in the spring, in 1562 and 1564 she was in Aberdeen and Inverness in the summer, she was in Argyll and Ayrshire in the summer of 1563, and in the autumn of 1565 and 1566 she was in the south-west and south. Her principal residence was Holyrood, but she spent some quite long periods at Stirling. Plenty of her subjects had the opportunity to say 'God bless that sweet face', and there is little doubt that by personality as well as policy she made herself acceptable to the great majority of her people.

Whether Mary could continue her successful rule did not depend on the political or ecclesiastial situation in Scotland. It depended on two other things which were inextricably bound up with each other – her relations with Elizabeth and her choice of a husband. It has been said that Scotland was nothing more to Mary than an 'interlude between the France of her memories and the England of her dreams'. If Mary was indeed pursuing her policy in Scotland because of its possible effect on her relations with England and other powers, the question was, could it yield the expected dividends? The international aspect of her policy was clear enough in the mind of at least one of her advisers, Maitland of Lethington, though no doubt Lord James concurred. Maitland, who was something of a sceptic in religion, thought of politics all the time, and if he had any enthusiasm at all in his calculating soul it was for the peaceful union of England and Scotland: in his view, therefore, Mary must be 'allured' into friendship with England through recognition as heir to Elizabeth in return for her renunciation of any claim to the English throne during Elizabeth's life.

It looks as if this policy had been agreed on before Mary left France, because within a fortnight of her arrival in Scotland Maitland was on his way to England to sound Elizabeth on the question of the succession. He at once encountered a difficulty which was to be persistent, namely Elizabeth's refusal to name her heir. Her excuse was that she would not hang her winding-sheet before her own eyes, and she has on the whole been applauded for the line she took, on the grounds that a designated successor would have attracted support and weakened her position. This, however, is an inadequate defence, for the majority of monarchs have known who their successors were to be and have not found it a great handicap. The allusion to the winding-sheet suggests rather the simple fact that, with her habitual irresolution and her weakness on long-term strategy, she simply could not bring herself to face the fact that one day she must die and have a successor. Her attitude was like that of Louis XV – 'after me the deluge' – and it was nothing to her that her death might be followed by a war of succession.

At this stage, in the autumn of 1561, Elizabeth countered Maitland's request with a demand that Mary should ratify the Treaty of Edinburgh, by which she had been obliged to lay aside the style and arms of a queen of England. This seemed reasonable, but the treaty's words were that Mary should abstain 'henceforward' from styling herself Queen of England, and this might be interpreted to preclude her from asserting her right to England even after Elizabeth's death. The Scottish answer, therefore, was that Mary would ratify the treaty if Elizabeth promised to acknowledge her as heir to England. What was implied – and what Maitland wanted – was a kind of mutual recognition between the two queens, whose interests were not necessarily opposed to each other. According to a contemporary, 'My Lord of Moray had great credit with my Lord Robert Dudley, who was afterwards made Earl of Leicester, and the Secretary, Lethington, had great credit with the Secretary Cecil. So those four packed up a close and sisterly friendship between the two queens', who for a time corresponded weekly. Mary reaffirmed her offer of mutual recognition in January 1562, when she suggested that she should meet Elizabeth in person. Arrangements were made for such a meeting, to take place at Nottingham on 3 September 1562, but Elizabeth intimated in July that she could not associate with a daughter of the house of Guise at a time when persecution of the Huguenots had been resumed in France, following the return of the Duke of Guise to power in the spring. It sounds rather a forced argument: if Elizabeth had been sincere, and not looking for excuses to avoid a meeting, she might have been more impressed by what Mary herself was currently doing than by what her kinsmen were doing in France. But in September, instead of meeting Mary, Elizabeth made a treaty with the Huguenots. The truth may well have been that Elizabeth could not bring herself to a decision even on such a matter as a personal interview and that she shrank from a confrontation which would assuredly lead to comparisons of their appearance and personality.

Mary and Elizabeth were never to meet face to face, but their relations as two women, and not only as two queens, coloured the negotiations between them. While Mary was perhaps more woman than queen, and Elizabeth more queen than woman, it is nevertheless true that Elizabeth's attitude to matrimony was shaped by her outlook as a woman. She must have reflected on the fate of her own mother and of the other wives of Henry VIII and may have concluded that the matrimonial bond was degrading for the wife. It may also be guessed that, perhaps because of certain incidents in her adolescence, she found the physical side of marriage repugnant. Whether there was any sincerity or realism in a single one of her many matrimonial projects remains a mystery, and she certainly showed little enthusiasm for the marriage of others – her maids of honour, for example, or her bishops. So far as Mary was concerned, Elizabeth's attitude was a kind of dog-in-the-manger one: as she did not want to marry, Mary must not be allowed to marry either. If this is going too far, it can at least be said that it was probably distasteful to Elizabeth that Mary should find a husband while she herself, nine years Mary's senior, remained a spinster.

Mary on her side, while she may not at this stage have had much greater enthusiasm for matrimony than Elizabeth, had the strongest reasons, both as woman and as queen, to find a husband. Her sights, after all, were set on the English throne, and to

gain it on Elizabeth's death but have no children to succeed her
would be a barren triumph. Besides, the longer Elizabeth remained unmarried the more likely it was that Mary would succeed her and therefore the more urgent that Mary should have
an heir who could carry on the succession. It is, however, less
than fair to see it as a personal issue for Mary. The verses which
had welcomed her to Scotland in 1561 contained exhortations
not only to good government and support for the reformed
religion, but to matrimony. Her subjects must have been no less
anxious to see her married than Elizabeth's were to see their
Queen married. Scotland's interest, which must have weighed
with Mary's advisers if not with her, demanded her marriage,
especially as there was probably no widespread enthusiasm
for the Hamiltons, who were next in line of succession.

If Elizabeth's bargaining counter was her ability to concede
or withhold Mary's right to succeed her, Mary's was her freedom of action in religion and matrimony. Her countenance for
the Scottish Protestants made a favourable impression in
England, and if she would not renounce her Mass for Scotland
she might perhaps be induced to do it for England: on the other
hand, she had not severed links with Rome, and could still
appeal to English Roman Catholics. Equally, the threat of a marriage to any enemy of England might bring pressure to bear on
Elizabeth. But, whatever Mary's personal wishes as a woman, her
problems in contemplating matrimony were mainly those of a
queen. The marriage of a queen regnant was a more delicate
question then than it is today, for her husband normally became king: Philip of Spain had lately been King of England as
the husband of Mary Tudor, and Francis II had been King of
Scots as the husband of Mary Stewart. To marry a subject and
raise him to the throne over his peers would certainly provoke
jealous discontent and perhaps civil war: even among the male
rulers of Scotland not one had made a subject his consort for
nearly two hundred years. A Roman Catholic husband would
upset the compromise Mary was maintaining in Scotland; a
Protestant husband would alienate her Roman Catholic friends
on the Continent and elsewhere. Marriage to a subject of another

sovereign was hardly consonant with Mary's dignity. Marriage to the sovereign, or the heir, of another kingdom raised its own problems: it would, at the least, introduce a foreign influence into the realm; what was worse, it might reopen the possibility of the kind of personal union from which Scotland had so recently escaped in the case of Francis II, and this would hardly be welcome to the Scots. These dangers seem, however, to have been little considered, and most of Mary's foreign suitors were in fact either sovereigns or the heirs of sovereigns: Charles IX of France, the Kings of Sweden and Denmark, the Archdukes Charles and Ferdinand (sons of the Emperor Charles V) and Don Carlos, son and heir of Philip II: the Prince of Condé was one of the few who were not. While almost any of those candidates might have been impolitic, none could be dismissed as wholly fanciful.

The Spanish negotiations were by far the most serious, and the motives behind them complex, for not all those who favoured them sincerely hoped that the marriage would take place. Moray and Maitland regarded the negotiations as a move in their deal-ings with England: Elizabeth, who could not fail to view a Spanish match, which would give Philip a base on her northern frontier, as a direct threat to her security, might be stimulated into ending her procrastination and making some counter-sug-gestion, including a recognition of Mary's claim as her heir. To Mary, marriage to Don Carlos would open the possibility of Spanish and papal help to oust Elizabeth without awaiting her death in the course of nature. The negotiations went on after a fashion until April 1564, but they ceased to be realistic by the end of 1563, for Don Carlos, who had all along been a poor creature physically and mentally, had an accident which finally made him hopelessly insane.

In June 1563 Elizabeth had told Maitland of Lethington that if Mary married Don Carlos she would be her enemy, whereas if she married to please her she would be acknowledged as heir to England. It was not unreasonable for the Scots to feel that if Elizabeth had any eye at all to the future of her own country she might well want to abandon her negative and obstructive attitude and make a positive suggestion of a suitable consort, who would, after all, presumably sire her own successors. This Elizabeth did, in a vague way as early as March 1563 and in definite terms a year later, but her suggestion was so startling as to be hardly credible. Her own favourite among Englishmen had long been Robert Dudley, a son of that Earl of Warwick and Duke of Northumberland who had been Protector in the later part of Edward VI's reign. There had been a good deal of scandal about Elizabeth and Dudley, and the sudden death of Dudley's wife, Amy Robsart, in September 1560, was believed to have been no accident, but a deliberate step to clear the way for Dudley's marriage to the Queen. Had Elizabeth in fact married Dudley after his wife's death she might well have met the fate which Mary herself was to meet when, in similar circumstances, she married Bothwell after Darnley's death. At that point Throckmorton, the English envoy in Paris, complained that people were asking him what kind of religion the English had, that a subject could kill his wife and the Queen not only condone the crime but marry the murderer.

It has been remarked that Elizabeth's offer of Dudley to Mary shows, more than any other incident, how far we are from understanding the working of the sixteenth-century mind. Dudley was only the younger son of a peer of recent creation, and it was not until after he had been offered to Mary that he was himself created Earl of Leicester (September 1564); besides, the past apart, his course with Elizabeth was by no means run, and it is hard to believe that she wanted to discard him. Was she vain enough to think that Mary would regard the offer as a mark of signal generosity, or did she make it in full confidence that it would be rejected and that she would then have a pretext for dismissing Mary's claims? It is a measure of the devotion of Mary's advisers to the English succession that they were prepared to consider even this match if it carried with it the desired concession, and negotiations went on until the beginning of 1565.

The next events, which actually led to Mary's marriage, were in a sense unexpected, and yet the marriage which took place was one that had been thought of many times before. Matthew Stewart, fourth Earl of Lennox, was a great-great-grandson of James II and had contested the right of his cousin, James Hamilton, second Earl of Arran, to be heir presumptive to Mary and Governor of the Realm in her minority. When Arran fell under the sway of the French party in 1543, Lennox had appealed to Henry VIII. His subsequent activities as an English agent had led to his forfeiture, and he had settled in England, where he married Margaret Douglas, daughter of Margaret Tudor, sister of Henry VIII. Thus the son of Lennox and Margaret Douglas, Henry Stewart, Lord Darnley, born in 1545, was going to have the next claim, at least after the Hamiltons, and perhaps before them, to the Scottish succession, and the next claim, at least after Mary, to the English succession; as Darnley had been brought up as an Englishman, some thought his claim to England superior to Mary's. The possibility of a marriage between him and Mary had been thought of almost from his birth, and had been revived after the death of Francis. If, then, Mary abandoned a foreign match and rejected Dudley, here was an obvious spouse.

It is difficult to eradicate the belief that the Lennoxes were Roman Catholics, but this is at best an over-simplification. Earl Matthew had worked for Henry VIII against the French and papalist faction in Scotland and had been associated with Somerset's operations in 1547–8, when an even more direct appeal had been made to Scots to join England in its stand against Rome. Later, in the minority of James VI, Lennox was to become Regent of Scotland on terms which would assuredly not have been acceptable except to a convinced Protestant. And his brother, the Bishop of Caithness, who shared a good part of the earl's English exile, was one of the three Scottish bishops who accepted the reformation and organized the reformed Church in their dioceses. Darnley himself, whom some thought 'indifferent in religion', had professed the reformed faith in England, and he absented himself from the nuptial Mass at his wedding. He did not scruple to attend the services conducted by John Knox in the church of St Giles and it was remarked in December

1565 that he had 'always shown himself a Protestant'. When, at a later stage, he did begin to attend Mass it was thought worthy of remark. However, his mother, who had that attachment to Rome which was characteristic of more women than men both in that century and the next, seems to have done her best to groom her son as a candidate for the English throne who would be acceptable to English Roman Catholics, and at one point she brought both her husband and herself under suspicion for trafficking with papists.

There could be little doubt about the implications of Lennox's return to Scotland, after twenty years of exile, in September 1564, and the annulment of his forfeiture by parliament in December. Darnley now had his father's presence in Scotland as a pretext for crossing the Border, and he arrived in Scotland in February 1565, with a passport valid for three months. When Mary had first seen this young man, at the coronation of Francis II in 1559, he had been only thirteen, and when he arrived in France again, after the death of Francis, the fifteen-year-old boy still made no impression on the eighteen-year-old widow. Now, however, Mary was at once attracted to 'the lustiest and best proportionit lang man that she had seen'. He was indeed tall, like the Queen herself, and good-looking in a soft kind of way; a contemporary Scot described him as 'more like a woman than a man, for he was handsome, beardless, and baby-faced', but Mary may have found his smooth mouth and cheeks more attractive than those of more hirsute Scottish nobles. Her susceptibilities may well have been intensified by the failure of the other marriage plans, for Darnley at least offered a practicable match. In fact, Darnley might have been the ideal husband if only he had had a brain to match his birth, but the Cardinal of Lorraine described him as *un gentil huteaudeau* – an agreeable nincompoop. Shortly after he arrived in Scotland he fell ill with measles, and as Mary nursed him she found her affection increasing: it has to be remembered that she had already nursed a husband through a painful and fatal illness, and there may have been a quasi-maternal element in her attitude to the immature-looking Darnley. At any rate, on the day he was able to leave his room (15 May) he was created Earl of Ross, and this was considered tantamount to a betrothal.

It has been said of an earlier Scottish royal marriage – that of James I to Joan Beaufort in 1423 – that 'romance found the match which policy would have dictated', and clearly from the point of view of Mary's claims to England a marriage to Darnley was politic, for it reinforced her own right with that of Darnley. The mystery is why Elizabeth permitted Darnley to go to Scotland and so facilitated a marriage which combined two claims to her throne. Not only did she permit Darnley's return, but she chose this point (mid-March) to intimate that the Dudley marriage would not bring Mary recognition as her heir and that she would not make any declaration about the succession until she herself had either married or had announced her resolve never to marry : this indicated that Mary had nothing to gain by trying to please Elizabeth in choosing a husband, and invited her to go her own way. From the English point of view, the one slight advantage Darnley offered was that he was preferable to a continental Roman Catholic. Characteristically enough, after Elizabeth had given Lennox permission to go to Scotland, she tried to withdraw her consent at the last moment, and after the marriage of Mary and Darnley had taken place she intimated her disapproval of it. She may possibly have calculated – if she calculated at all – that as the Lennoxes had lands in England and as Lady Lennox was still there, she retained a hold over them, and she actually sent the countess to the Tower. Elizabeth may perhaps have been subtle and malevolent enough to assess Darnley's character and conclude that he would bring nothing save misery to her 'sister queen'. But she may merely have welcomed a plausible pretext for dashing Mary's hopes of a declaration on the succession. Mary, at any rate, thought her ostensible opposition was insincere.

But if the marriage was politic in Mary's eyes in relation to her English claims, it was not so politic in relation to the situation in Scotland. The anglicized Lennoxes, with their treasonable record, can hardly have been popular, and it was not only their dynastic rivals, the Hamiltons, who looked askance at the eleva-

tion of a Lennox to the position of King Consort. When proclamation was made that the government would in future be
carried on in the names of 'Henry and Mary, King and Queen
of Scots', no one besides Lennox cried, 'God save His Grace.'
The one other earl to whom Darnley's elevation may have had
some appeal was Morton, head of the house of Douglas during
the minority of the Earl of Angus (whose tutor he was), for
Darnley was the grandson of an Earl of Angus, and his mother,
Margaret Douglas, in May 1565 renounced her claim to the
earldom of Angus, so ensuring the position of Morton's protégé.
The marriage (on 29 July 1565) was according to the Roman
rite, and Mary, professing her willingness to defend 'the Catholic
religion', had applied to the Pope for the dispensation necessary to enable her to marry her first cousin, though the marriage
took place before the dispensation arrived.

Mary did her best to reassure her Protestant subjects. She
professed to be ready to hear discussions about the Scriptures
and even to attend public preaching, she issued a proclamation
reiterating that members of the reformed Church would not
be molested because of their faith, and she later reissued her
original proclamation forbidding any alteration in the state of
religion. Suspicions were not entirely allayed, and could be
appealed to by those to whom the Queen's actions were distasteful for political reasons. The men who really suffered by the
Queen's marriage to Darnley were Moray and Maitland, for
their whole policy had been founded on the prospect of an
accommodation with Elizabeth, and such a prospect was now at
an end. Besides, since Mary's return Moray had seen his possible rivals – Arran, Bothwell, and Huntly – in turn eliminated
from the possibility of influencing the Queen, while he, it
seemed, had become indispensable. Now his place at her side
might be taken by an empty-headed fop of nineteen and anyone
this newcomer might choose.

Yet, while the reasons for Moray's chagrin are obvious
enough, it is hard to see what he hoped to achieve by raising a
rebellion. He had come to power once before as the result of the
revolution of 1559–60, carried through with English help against

Mary of Guise. He was to return to power once more, in 1567, as a result of a revolution against Mary Stewart, carried through without English help. But at this stage he had no real case against the Queen to justify rebellion. Mary's equitable church policy was such as to wean a large number of former Lords of the Congregation from his side, and almost the only consti-tutional ground for complaint was that Darnley had been raised to kingship without parliamentary authority. To take up arms after Mary had actually married Darnley was particularly inept, for the Queen could hardly be separated from her lawful hus-band. Possibly, if English help had been forthcoming and if Moray had received wider Scottish support, some kind of coun-cil might have been imposed on Mary, but that would have been all. As it was, although English help was promised it was never given, at least on any effective scale, while Mary, on her side, strengthened her position by restoring the heir of Huntly and recalling the Earl of Bothwell. Behind this was the popularity Mary had built up since her return nearly four years earlier: she was a vastly different opponent from the middle-aged dowager with whom Moray had had to contend in 1559–60.

When military operations began, Mary showed a resolution worthy of her forefathers. Her remark that she wished she had been a man, to lie out in the fields all night, parallels Elizabeth's speech at Tilbury: 'I know I have the body of a weak and feeble woman, but I have the heart and stomach of a king, and of a King of England too.' In March Moray had made a bond with Argyll and Châtelherault, but the rebellion did not begin until August. When the rebels gathered at Ayr, the Queen ordered a muster (22 August) and pledged her jewels to pay soldiers. On 26 August she left Edinburgh for the west, and although the rebels evaded her and entered Edinburgh on 31 August, they met with such a cool reception that they withdrew on 2 Septem-ber and on 6 September they were in Dumfries, where they awaited English help. Mary had meanwhile returned to the capital to raise a larger force, but it proved to be unnecessary. English help for the insurrection was not forthcoming and on 6 October Moray crossed the Border, to learn that while Elizabeth had encouraged him in his rising she had no room for failures and wholly repudiated him. The whole rebellion had been little more than one of those bloodless demonstrations in which sixteenth-century Scots were practised.

While the failure of the rebellion had shown that Mary's policy had gained support, the circumstances of its occurrence and successful suppression reacted on her attitude. For one thing, there no longer seemed any hope of winning Elizabeth. Not only had that Queen made it clear that she regarded the Darnley marriage as an act of hostility, but the countenance she had given to the rebels – despite her subsequent disavowals – was a clear intimation that she was the enemy of the Scottish régime. Equally, all Mary's amiability towards the Protestants had neither won friendship in England nor averted rebellion at home. She might have been excused for feeling that all her detachment in ecclesiastical matters, all her concessions to the reformers, had been unprofitable and that the time had come to lean on the more conservative elements in the hope that they would prove more reliable than the friends of England and the Reformation. Archbishop Hamilton was set free, and the administration of the thirds of benefices, previously in the hands of Wishart of Pittarro, an 'earnest professor' of the gospel, was now committed to Murray of Tullibardine, who was more complaisant to the demands of the Crown. While this made Mary more than ever dependent on revenues drawn from the Church's wealth, the inroads now made by the Crown on the thirds were gravely prejudicial to the reformed Church, and it was soon to be complained, with some truth, that 'the ministers' stipends could not be paid'. Besides, after being confronted by a Protestant revolt, Mary could the more easily assume the role of a suffering Catholic: she asked for aid, on religious grounds, from Philip of Spain, and she sent the Bishop of Dunblane to Rome to ask for men and money on her behalf, while she professed her intention to take parliamentary action for 'the auld religion'. It might be argued that at this point Mary, freed from the tutelage of Moray, was pursuing a policy more after her own heart, and it is true that she had some initiative: but it is not so clear that she had real freedom of action. If there was a deliberate change of policy the motive was nonetheless as opportunist as ever. She said in December 1565 that she would not adhere to Protestantism and thereby risk losing her continental friends when she had 'no assurance of anything that may countervail the same' – in other words, no guarantee from Elizabeth.

Mary had already been accused by Moray and his associates of 'leaving the wholesome advice and counsel' of her nobles and barons and following instead that of 'such men, strangers, as have neither judgment nor experience of the ancient laws and governance of this realm' and were 'of base degree, and seeking nothing but their own commodities'. This had not been true hitherto, but now, with her changed policy, Mary found that there were few peers on whom she could rely and there had to be new men as well as new measures. Most of the Protestants who had not supported Moray's rebellion were now alienated by Mary's apparent leanings towards Rome, as well as by the shelving of the policy of amity with England. The only earls who were regularly about her were Huntly, Bothwell, Atholl, and Lennox: the last was the King's father, Atholl had voted against the Protestant legislation of 1560, Huntly inherited something of the conservative tradition of his house and was grateful to Mary for restoring to him his father's forfeited properties, and Bothwell, though a strong Protestant, always put loyalty to the Queen first. Mary was therefore driven to rely more than before on men of lower birth, some of whom happened to be foreigners, and attention fastened at the time, as it has fastened ever since, on David Riccio.

Riccio was a Savoyard who had come to Scotland in 1561 in the train of the ambassador from Savoy, and it was his musical accomplishments that first brought him to Mary's notice. He was soon conspicuous by his constant presence in the Queen's innermost circle, and at first after her marriage he was an intimate associate of Darnley. He became a secretary on the establishment which Mary maintained as Queen Dowager of France, but he was not, as so often said, appointed Secretary of

State, and there is no foundation for the idea, put about by his enemies at the time, that it was intended to deprive Morton of the Great Seal and make the Italian Chancellor. Nor is there evidence to support the protestant suspicion that he was a papal agent. But the situation was serious enough. A preference for men of humbler birth had helped to bring about the downfall of Mary's father, foreigners were never popular, and it had not been forgotten that the 'Concessions' granted in the names of Francis and Mary in 1560 forbade the employment of foreigners in public office in Scotland. Nobles and others found that their applications to the Queen had to pass through the hands of Riccio, who adopted a haughty attitude not in keeping with his origins.

There was, however, another element, besides jealousy of a foreigner, in the events which led to Riccio's murder. It had not taken Mary long to see that Darnley was utterly unfitted for a share of political power, and that playboy was too addicted to his amusements – hunting, hawking, music, and women – to give much attention to government. There is little evidence that he was deliberately excluded from business, but much that he had little taste for attending to it; and the consequence was that in time he was ignored and a stamp used for his signature. It would have been quite inappropriate to grant him the 'crown matrimonial' on terms which would have given sovereignty to him and his heirs should Mary predecease him without issue. Although his situation was of his own making, he was very dissatisfied. He was the grandson of that 'young witless fool', the sixth Earl of Angus, who had married a queen at nineteen or thereabouts, but he may have felt some sensitiveness as a parvenu. Admittedly, he was descended from both Scottish and English kings, but his Tudor blood was that of upstarts, while Mary had been a Queen of France and the Guises boasted descent from Charlemagne. At any rate, his feeling was that he was debarred from political influence, while men like Riccio advised the Queen. The idea also took shape in his mind, or was implanted there by other enemies of Riccio, that the Italian was the father of the child of whom Mary became pregnant in the autumn of 1565. This suspicion is hardly credible and, while contemporaries long jested about it, it is not so clear that even they believed it. It is much more likely that Mary went no farther than the dictates of her natural kindness towards her dependants and a perfectly intelligible liking for the society of a congenial and entertaining servant. But both the King Consort and the lords who were irked by the prominence of Riccio saw the Italian as the individual who was in one way or another supplanting them in the Queen's favour, and there was an obvious basis for a conspiracy.

While a number of the leaders of Moray's rebellion had been pardoned, others, including Moray himself, Argyll, Glencairn, Rothes, Ochiltree, Boyd, and Kirkcaldy of Grange, were summoned to stand trial for treason at a parliament which was to meet on 7 March and proceed to their Attainder on the 12th. These notables, along with Morton and others who had not been in their rebellion but had been alienated by Mary's proceedings since, agreed to support Darnley's demand for the crown matrimonial on condition that he would prevent action against them. This alliance was a striking commentary on the prevailing lack of principle: Moray and his fellows had raised their rebellion in protest against the marriage to Darnley, yet now they were conspiring to give him a position the Queen denied him.

The murder of Riccio was a mere incident in the plot, and it is only too evident that the Italian himself was far too small game to merit a large-scale conspiracy. He was, it is true, a focus for various discontents, but there was no need to make a public spectacle of his liquidation. The truth seems to be that the design was much more sinister. The attack on Riccio was carried out, on 9 March 1566, with quite unnecessary violence and brutality in Mary's presence, and the intention clearly was to threaten the lives of the Queen and her unborn child. The formal indictment of the murderers stated that they had put violent hands on the Queen and had given her occasion 'by sight of the said cruel slaughter and by the thrusting of her person in violent manner to part with her birth'. Mary might easily have been killed in the confusion of the tiny and crowded supper-chamber.

A pistol was actually held against her body, and when the table was overturned only the presence of mind of the Countess of Argyll, who seized a candle, prevented the room from being plunged into gloom relieved only by flickering fire-light. Talk both before and after the murder suggests that the death of the Queen was within the calculations of the conspirators: on 13 February it had been reported that something was intended against her, and after the crime it was reported on the Continent that Darnley had murdered his wife. The ringleaders in the events at Holyrood were Morton, Lindsay, and Ruthven, and they showed their Protestant zeal by murdering a Dominican friar whom Mary was harbouring, but the devious Moray and his associates were nearby, ready to enter Edinburgh as soon as the deed was done.

Not only did the design against Mary fail, for she survived the ordeal and matched her physical courage with intelligence even in this crisis, but the other parts of the plot were only partly successful. The intended proceedings of parliament were cancelled, so saving the estates of the rebels of the previous year from forfeiture, but Mary, who knew Darnley well enough to realize that he was the weak link in the chain, succeeded by her blandishments in detaching him from his allies and escaping with him from Holyrood to Dunbar early on 12 March. Darnley's dagger had been carefully left in Riccio's corpse, and his associates now sent Mary the bond which proved his complicity, but they had lost their game and did not regain power. They thought it prudent to leave Edinburgh on the morning of 17 March; and John Knox, who had warmly applauded the murder and was an expert in detecting danger, departed later the same day for the safety of Ayrshire.

Mary was triumphant, but she saw that her position was based on the support of too small a number of notables. She still had with her some of her non-aristocratic familiars, notably Sir James Balfour (who became Clerk Register), but at first only her old friends Huntly, Atholl, and Bothwell, with Fleming and Seton, joined her at Dunbar. She could, however, appeal to generally conservative peers like Home, Marischal, Caithness,

Cassillis, Crawford, and Sutherland. The Hamiltons, too, had been pardoned in January for their part in the Chaseabout Raid. She now made a good tactical move and split the opposition by offering pardons to the others involved in the Chaseabout rising, as distinct from the murderers of Riccio. On 18 March she was back in Edinburgh with a force said to number 8,000 men. Next day the privy council summoned the leading murderers and more than sixty other persons to appear within six days; but they had already crossed to England. Moray, Glencairn, and Argyll, now restored to favour, were reconciled to Huntly, Bothwell, and Atholl, with whom they formed the core of the administration for almost a year. Yet this coalition was probably inherently unstable, for there can have been little trust among men of such divergent views, and, one would think, little trust by the Queen herself in Moray, Glencairn, and Argyll. It should be said that the parliament of 1566 passed some sound legislation, which suggests that good government was being carried on.

Mary's child was born in Edinburgh Castle on 19 June 1566. The notion that her baby died at birth and that the future James VI was a substitute, perhaps a son of the Earl of Mar, is one that is constantly resurrected by those who prefer mysteries to the truth, but it has little to support it. The alleged 'coffin in the wall', containing the skeleton of an infant wrapped in cloth with the royal monogram, dissolves on examination into some unmarked and indeterminate bones, perhaps not even human bones. Besides, Archbishop Hamilton was in the castle at the time, and it may be taken as certain that he would use his official position, in the interests of his house, to ensure that there was no substitution of one child for another. In any event, James in his youth showed such a marked physical resemblance to Darnley that both the Riccio scandal and the supposed coffin in the wall can be dismissed. The birth of the prince did nothing to strengthen Mary's position. For one thing, he was likely to be brought up in his mother's religion, which opened the prospect of a succession of Roman Catholic sovereigns – like the birth of another Prince James in another June one hundred and twenty-two years later; secondly, Mary's own life was no longer the sole barrier against the likelihood of a disputed succession; and, thirdly, the accession of an infant sovereign would offer great opportunities to those who, whether from policy or ambition, could make capital out of a minority. Darnley, who no longer saw the way to power through the crown matrimonial, could calculate that he might hope to control his son should Mary die.

It is hard to believe that Mary's reconciliation with Darnley, after Riccio's murder, can have been sincere: how could it be if she realized that he had sought her life and that of her child? It is true that, in the inventory of her possessions drawn up shortly before the prince's birth, when Mary was probably eager to be in love and charity with all, the number of articles bequeathed to Darnley was at least fifteen and may have been as high as twenty-six. Yet before the end of April there had been a report of a mission to Rome to seek a divorce, and although Darnley did come to see the new-born prince, and gave Mary an opportunity to pronounce solemnly that the infant was his – so much his that she feared it would be the worse for the child hereafter – their subsequent relations were unhappy, except perhaps for a time in September. It is quite clear that they seldom – some thought never – cohabited again after the prince's birth and that they certainly did not do so after September at the latest. It was common knowledge that Mary found her husband repulsive. 'It cannot for modesty, nor with the honour of a Queen, be repeated what she said of him', wrote an English envoy, the Earl of Bedford.

It may be that Mary's principal care, in the anxious months before the birth of her son, had been to find someone utterly honest and reliable and at the same time highly placed and capable. If, irked by the behaviour of Darnley and conscious of perils threatening her from every side, she was looking for the support of a man of assured loyalty, then the strongest candidate was the thirty-year-old James Hepburn, Earl of Bothwell. Although he had early been converted to Protestantism, the cause of the Crown came first with him, and, as a trusted supporter of Mary of Guise, he had brought off one good *coup* against the Lords of the Congregation, when he intercepted money on its way to them from England. Patriotism was as potent with Bothwell as loyalty, for he was said to be 'as mortal an enemy to the English as any man alive'. Described as 'rash and vainglorious', he was not the most peaceful of subjects, and when out of favour early in Mary's personal reign he went (not for the first time) to France, where he became Captain of the Scottish Archers. He was no ruffian, but a cultivated man familiar with the ways of courts, and his sister married Lord John Stewart, who was probably Mary's favourite among her half-brothers.

Bothwell's family, the Hepburns of Hailes, were one of the most important in south-eastern Scotland, with wide lands of their own and wider influence through their leadership of other Hepburn families. They were hereditary High Admirals of Scotland, and usually held many other offices as well: Earl Patrick, James's father, had been Lieutenant of the Borders, and Earl James, appointed by Mary of Guise to succeed him, was re-

appointed to this important office by Queen Mary in September
1565; Earl James was also Sheriff of the three Lothians and
Bailie of Lauderdale. He could muster many hard-fighting Borderers, and he had raised a force of them on Mary's behalf after
the Riccio murder. His own castles of Borthwick, Crichton, and
Hailes dominated much of Mid and East Lothian and he was
master also of the great fortress of Hermitage, which commanded the western marches. In March 1566 he received the lands
and lordship of Dunbar, with the office of keeper of its sea-girt
castle, which, situated on the open sea just outside the Firth of
Forth, was an important communication point with the Continent. The Hepburns, like others, had been acquisitive of
ecclesiastical property : they had long regarded the properties
of the nunnery of Haddington as at their disposal, they had an
interest in the abbey of Melrose, and on 30 June 1566 the nunnery of North Berwick was conferred on Earl James – like the
gift of Dunbar a reward for his services and a sign of his growing favour in the eyes of the Queen.

But was Mary looking for more than loyalty and for more
than a faithful servant in the shape of a reliable soldier and
official? She had not been indifferent to men : she had loved
Francis, she had given encouragement to Young Arran, she had
loved Darnley. So far as her private life was concerned, she
had been married when she was fifteen and she knew, or ought to
have known, that the utmost discretion was expected of the wife
of a prince. Besides, when she was in France Mary spent a good
deal of time not at court but at the country house of her Guise
grandmother, who was a model of rectitude, if not severity, in
her moral outlook. A very capable woman, and proud of her
family's position, the duchess, who had taken a great interest
in Mary from the time of her arrival in France, had no taste for
frivolity. But if propriety had been instilled into Mary, she had
also learned that, as the marriages of princesses were commonly
dictated by political expediency, they had to curb their pas-
sions. It was Mary's good fortune that with Young Arran, as
with Francis and Darnley, expediency and affection had happily

combined. Did they or did they not combine once more with Bothwell?

There had been episodes in Mary's earlier reign in Scotland which, if they do not show passion on her side, show that some of her subjects did not forget she was a woman and which are instructive for the light they may throw on later events. The first of them brought together in a somewhat mysterious way Mary's former suitor Young Arran and her future husband the Earl of Bothwell. There was a sudden alarm at the court in November 1561, apparently arising from a remark of Arran that it would be no difficult matter to 'take her out of the abbey' (that is, the palace of Holyroodhouse), and in the following spring Arran accused Bothwell of suggesting that the Queen should be seized and carried off to the Hamilton stronghold of Dumbarton. It was evident that Arran's obsession with his hopes of marrying Mary, so often frustrated, had caused his mind to become unhinged. Other men were to lose their lives for the love of Mary, but Arran was the only one who lost his wits. He was confined until his death in 1609, when, rather touchingly, it was recalled that he had been noted for his 'good and godly zeal . . . in the defence of God's cause'. His ally Bothwell, who was held to be compromised, was imprisoned and banished, and the affair was taken seriously enough to lead to the institution of a bodyguard to protect the Queen.

The second episode was one aspect of Mary's relations with Huntly's family, which led to the battle of Corrichie in 1562. Sir John Gordon, Huntly's son, although he already had a wife whom he kept in concealment, was believed to have designs on the Queen. One of the accusations against Huntly was that he had conspired to help his son to enter the Queen's lodging with a great number of armed men and to desire 'such things of Her Highness as were not lawful' and, in case of her refusal, 'to put violent hands on her person and lead her where they pleased'. Mary herself seems to have believed that this charge was not without foundation.

The third episode concerned the French poet Châtelard, a descendant of the Chevalier Bayard, who had accompanied Mary from France in 1561 and came to Scotland again in November 1562. The censorious thought that the Queen was unduly familiar with him, and Knox went so far as to say that 'the Queen would lie upon Châtelard's shoulder, and sometimes privily she would steal a kiss of his neck.' Châtelard evidently thought he had sufficient encouragement from Mary to hide one night under her bed, where he was found by two grooms making their customary search. A couple of days later he intruded into Mary's chamber when only some of her ladies were there. After the first escapade Mary had forbidden him her presence: after the second he was executed.

These incidents suggest that Mary was not as remote or secluded as might be thought, and that she might conceivably have been accessible to a lover; they also show that the possibility of seizing her by force was not one to be dismissed as wildly impracticable. And it is a little odd that the Earl of Bothwell, who was alleged to have entered into a plot to carry Mary off to Dumbarton in Arran's interest in 1562, did eventually carry her off to Dunbar in his own interest in 1567.

But, while Mary was not indifferent to men, there is nothing to suggest that she had been deeply moved by sexual passion. Her conduct of public affairs, with all its opportunism and calculation, indicates not only intelligence but a detachment which a woman of passionate nature could hardly have shown. There had been little to suggest strong emotion at all, and, leaving aside the improbable scandal about Riccio – even though it showed that people believed that a man could have access to her – Mary had kept her reputation all but unspotted. However, after the traumatic experience of her troubled pregnancy and her difficult parturition her emotional nature may have undergone a change.

On Bothwell's side there was probably no ambiguity. He had, of course, met Mary in France before she came to Scotland, but at that stage she had no attraction for him. She might have a handsome appearance, but there was a certain fragility too, with her intermittent ill-health, and she was too young and immature to appeal to his robust manhood. Now, however, after her marriage to Darnley and her experience of maternity, she was awakened emotionally and in her new maturity was attractive to Bothwell as never before. Not only was Bothwell personally notorious as a womanizer, schooled as he was by his reprobate great-uncle, the Bishop of Moray, who boasted of having had a dozen mistresses, seven of them men's wives, but one element in his family heritage was a habit of what was euphemistically called 'kindness' to widowed queens, and since the death of James I in 1437 there had hardly been a royal relict whose name had not been linked with the Hepburn of Hailes of her day. Earl James's own father, Patrick, was one of the gentlemen with whom Mary of Guise was thought to have 'over-great familiarity', and in 1543 he had procured a divorce with a view to marrying the Dowager Queen. Earl James had married Jane Gordon, sister of the Earl of Huntly, in February 1566, but it did not require much originality for him to reflect that he might divorce her and marry the Queen if she were quit of her husband.

At the same time, contemporary evidence of a love affair between Bothwell and Mary before Darnley's death is non-existent, for the familiar tales of their scandalous proceedings are the inventions of George Buchanan. His stories, detailed and circumstantial as some of them seem, generally have elements of improbability and can often be shown to be contrary to authentic fact. For example, Buchanan would have it that when Mary made her will in June 1566 she showed her favour to Bothwell and her contempt for Darnley, whereas the surviving document contains at least fifteen bequests to Darnley and only two to Bothwell. One of the many improbabilities related by Buchanan is that in September 1566, when Mary was living in a house adjoining the exchequer office in Edinburgh to attend to financial business, Bothwell frequently visited her from an adjoining dwelling. On one occasion, when he did not keep an appointment, she sent Lady Reres to take him out of the bed where he lay with his wife and bring him to her: but Lady Reres is described by Buchanan himself as elderly and corpulent, and this made her an unlikely candidate for climbing over a wall (according to one version) or being let down by a sash into the next garden (according to another).

Perhaps the best known of Buchanan's fabrications relates to what happened in October 1566, when Mary was at Jedburgh administering justice, and Bothwell, after being seriously injured in a Border skirmish, was lying ill in his castle of Hermitage. The tale goes that the Queen immediately set out to visit her lover, with disreputable company and in winter weather, but the truth is that five or six days elapsed between Mary's receiving the news (which she probably did before she reached Jedburgh) and her visit to Hermitage. October is not exactly the heart of winter, and Mary's entourage on her ride included the Earl of Moray, whom it was careless of his client Buchanan to class as one of the 'thieves and traitors' who accompanied her. The ride to Hermitage and back was made in one day, because there was no domestic staff at Hermitage to cope with a Queen's visit, and it did bring on the most serious of Mary's many illnesses: on 25 October she was thought to be dead. After recovering and making a circuit of the eastern Border, she spent a fortnight, from 20 November, at Craigmillar, near Edinburgh, and then a few days at Holyrood before going to Stirling for the baptism of the prince on 17 December.

Just as Buchanan has misled over the details of Mary's association with Bothwell, so he has misled by singling out Bothwell as the one villain from whose initiative subsequent events arose. While Bothwell had his own motives, other men, who had no idea of profiting from the Queen's release from her marriage, could nevertheless see that her relationship with her husband now represented a major problem. Darnley had withdrawn from the court in September and had been talking of going abroad, complaining that he was deprived of any royal authority, was deserted by the nobles, and despised by his wife. He did not accompany Mary on her tour in the south, and, although he ultimately came to her sick-bed at Jedburgh, the convalescent Bothwell had anticipated him by several days. The royal pair met again on two or three occasions within the following few weeks, but neither made any attempt to conceal

that their estrangement was complete. Darnley did not attend
the baptism, though he was in Stirling Castle at the time,
and the arrangements were made by Bothwell. It was only at
this late stage, when Darnley had proved utterly intolerable,
that he was finally ignored in the conduct of business and had
to be content with an inadequate allowance. He retired from
Stirling to Glasgow, a centre of his family's influence, where he
may have felt safer from the enemies he had unquestionably
made and where he was well placed for leaving the country
or for communicating with foreign powers. Mary's misery was
alluded to by the French ambassador, who said on 2 December
that she was

in the hands of physicians, and I do assure you is not at all well;
and I do believe the principal part of her disease to consist in a deep
grief and sorrow. . . . Still she repeats these words, 'I could wish to
be dead'.

Loyalty to Mary might have stimulated some of her politicians and courtiers to action against Darnley, but equally an
ostensible regard for the Queen's service might be a cloak for
others who were less disinterested. Even before his marriage,
when Darnley had already made himself unpopular by his
childish arrogance, the English ambassador remarked, 'I know
not, but it is greatly to be feared that he can have no long life
among these people.' In May 1566, less than a year after the marriage, Argyll and Moray had 'such misliking of their King as
never was more of man'. The conclusion was that 'such a young
fool and proud tyrant should not reign nor bear rule over them
and that he should be put off by one way or another'. During
Mary's stay at Craigmillar at the end of November, Bothwell,
Huntly, Argyll, Moray and Maitland of Lethington had conferred in her presence about her relations with her husband.
They offered that if Mary would pardon the Riccio murderers,
some means would be found to bring her marriage to an end.
Mary was hesitant about a divorce – or rather a decree of nullity
– lest it should make her son illegitimate, and Maitland of
Lethington hinted at other 'means' whereby she might be quit

of Darnley without prejudice to her son. She stipulated that nothing should be done contrary to her honour and conscience, and Maitland assured her that she would 'see nothing but good and approved by parliament'.

But it must have been clear that, whereas if Darnley were first divorced he might then be charged with treason and perhaps killed in resisting arrest, it was hardly possible to take any legal action against him as long as he was King, and the only option was violence. While it is not in the nature of conspirators to leave clear traces behind them, various pieces of evidence make it plain that Moray, Argyll, Huntly, Bothwell, and Maitland of Lethington were associated in a bond or bonds aimed at Darnley. They may not have had the Queen's approval or participation, but some of the evidence for their association and for the 'Craigmillar conference' comes from a document drawn up on Mary's behalf after she was in exile in England in 1568, and this makes it clear that she had been aware of schemes against her husband which might be sinister or criminal.

Mary's own actions in December 1566 seem in any event to put it beyond any reasonable doubt that she was not ignorant of such schemes. She suddenly showed an unprecedented generosity to the reformed Church, which had for some time been in a state of penury owing to the diversion to the Crown of an undue proportion of the thirds of benefices. Already in October there had been an ordinance that benefices worth less than £200 per annum should go to ministers; now, on 20 December, the Church received from the Queen a direct grant of £10,000 in money, with victual worth almost as much again, and in succeeding months ecclesiastical properties in burghs were made over to town councils. This looks like an attempt to buy support in a crisis which the Queen could foresee, and it is hard to believe that the divorce or death of Darnley would in itself produce a revulsion of feeling which she felt it necessary to forestall. On 23 December the Archbishop of St Andrews was formally restored to jurisdiction which would enable him to pronounce decrees of nullity between Mary and Darnley and between Bothwell and his wife. On 24 December Mary pardoned the Riccio murderers, who were thirsting for revenge on Darnley, and those who had sought their pardon must have been aware of the implications of their return. Although there is no evidence that Mary herself had at last agreed to concede the pardon in return for a specific undertaking to dispose of Darnley, Bothwell was not alone in seeing the event as a step towards 'a mark of his own that he shot at'. Before 9 January the commission to the archbishop had been revoked, and this might suggest that a plan other than divorce had by that time been selected to deal with Darnley.

But it would be a gross over-simplification to think solely of either the enemies of Darnley or a queen and her loyal subjects seeking, by fair means or foul, to bring to an end a union which had become intolerable. Mary herself was in danger, and some of her subjects were not loyal. Despite the financial concessions to the reformed Church, its wholehearted goodwill had not been secured. The prince was baptized by Roman Catholic rites – omitting only the spittle, on the insistence of Mary, who would not permit 'a pocky priest' (Archbishop Hamilton) to spit in her child's mouth; and although bishops had never been formally deprived of their consistorial jurisdiction and had continued since 1560 to exercise it occasionally, the grant of the commission to the archbishop was an act of defiance not only of the reformed Church but also of the commissary court which had been set up by Mary's own government in 1564 to deal with matrimonial cases. In that same month of December, Mary entered her twenty-fifth year, the year in which a Scottish sovereign was accustomed to make a revocation of grants of property made in his earlier years: the unpopularity of this proceeding had contributed to the downfall of James V, it was to contribute to the downfall of Charles I, and acquisitive nobles, dreading a revocation, may have made up their minds that Mary must not be allowed to complete the year she had just entered. Besides, should Mary be replaced, a royal minority offered fresh opportunities to the acquisitive and self-seeking.

The bald facts relating to Darnley's death are as follows. He had fallen ill at Glasgow, probably of syphilis, and had taken to his bed on Christmas Eve. Mary went to Glasgow and spent five days with him. Then, at the end of January, she brought him to Edinburgh and lodged him in a house on the outskirts of the town, in fact abutting on the town wall. Known as 'the old Provost's Lodging', it stood at the south-east corner of a quadrangular range of buildings which had been the residential quarters of the clergy of the collegiate church of St Mary in the Fields, on a site now occupied by the Old College of Edinburgh University. During Darnley's ten-day stay, Mary twice spent the night in the room beneath his, and was expected to sleep there again on the night of 9–10 February, but did not do so. About 2 o'clock on the morning of the 10th the building was demolished by an explosion. Two of Darnley's servants were found dead in the ruins, and one survived because he had been in a gallery which projected on to the town wall itself. The bodies of Darnley and his valet were found in the garden, outside the wall, with no external sign of any injury, but whereas Darnley was clad in only his night-shirt, the servant wore a cap and one slipper as well as his shirt, and beside the bodies lay a dressing-gown, a belt and dagger, a chair, and an indeterminate article which may have been a quilt.

By bringing Darnley to Edinburgh, Mary initiated the events which led directly to his death, but whether she was the agent of intending murderers is quite another matter. Her antipathy to her husband was not likely to have diminished, and on 20 January she expressed not only detestation of him but an accusation that he was plotting to do her some mischief, to crown Prince James, and assume the government. Yet on the same day she set out for Glasgow with the intention of bringing Darnley back to Edinburgh. It is in any event hard to believe that the many powerful men who wanted to kill Darnley could have thought of no other device than to use his wife as a decoy to entice him to Edinburgh. The simplest explanation of Mary's action is that she suddenly feared that she was pregnant of a child which everyone knew could not be her husband's and that it was therefore imperative to achieve a reconciliation with him.

There might be a more innocent reason why Mary should have enticed Darnley to Edinburgh, namely that she might thus have frustrated his plots and perhaps prevented him from going abroad, though his presence in, say, Spain, would have been far more embarrassing to England than to Scotland; but this possible design would not account for Mary's sudden change of attitude on 20 January. It would rather seem that, far from luring Darnley to his doom, Mary's interest now was to preserve his life at least long enough for them to resume marital relations. This would explain, as political motives do not, why, after Darnley was installed at Kirk o' Field, Mary went out of her way to play the part of a loving wife, visiting him every day, twice spending the night in a room beneath his, giving him a ring, and promising to sleep with him as soon as his convalescence was complete, which it would have been on the very day he was murdered.

On the theory that Mary feared she was pregnant, then, when she brought Darnley to Kirk o' Field, his death there was the last thing she wanted. The evidence about Mary's possible pregnancy at this time is conflicting. By June 1567 she was reported to be five months pregnant, and it has been argued on medical grounds that the twins of which she miscarried on 24 July must have been conceived long before her marriage to Bothwell in May. On the other hand, it has been suggested – rather desperately – that the report in June contained an error of 'months' for 'weeks', and, more convincingly, that she could not possibly have carried a child for five months without detection. It is worth noting not only that Mary had mistakenly believed herself to be pregnant during her first marriage but that she believed her pregnancy of James to have started a month before it can actually have done: she wrote on 2 April 1566 in a letter to Archbishop Beaton that she had been nearly seven months pregnant when Riccio was murdered on 9 March, whereas she was only approaching the completion of her sixth month. She may have miscalculated again, and the fear of a pregnancy – possibly stimulated by a sense of guilt after she had yielded to temptation – might account for the action in January, though a real pregnancy will be postulated to explain her actions after Darnley's death.

According to the indictment which was drawn up in the course of the investigations held after Mary had fled to England in 1568, the place of Darnley's residence in Edinburgh had been selected by Mary and Bothwell before he left Glasgow, and on his arrival in Edinburgh he was lodged in a building which from its situation and condition was no place of security. Mary's room, where she was expected to spend the night of 9–10 February, was beneath Darnley's; powder was placed in it, and on the fatal night she suddenly remembered that she had promised to be present at a masque at Holyrood in honour of the wedding of one of her servants. She therefore left Darnley and returned to Holyrood, whence Bothwell, after conferring with her, went to Kirk o' Field to fire the powder and blow up the King's lodging.

This artless tale is open to various objections. It seems that Mary's original intention was that Darnley should go to Craigmillar, and, while one account says that the destination was changed because he 'had no will' to go there, and other accounts say that he himself chose Kirk o' Field, the truth is uncertain. It seems a little unlikely that he himself would make the final choice, and there is some indication that when he arrived at Kirk o' Field he still did not know in which house he was going to take up residence. If, however, Kirk o' Field was Mary's choice, there was still nothing suspicious about it, for it was in a high, open situation, much more healthy than low-lying Holyrood. Nor can the old Provost's Lodging have been, as Mary's enemies later suggested, 'unmeet for an honest man to lodge in' and 'ruinous and waste', if it was considered a fit lodging for Mary herself.

Nor does it seem possible that the explosion was caused simply by powder in the Queen's room. The explosion completely wrecked, from the foundations upwards, a solidly constructed stone building, and the immediate thought of contemporaries was that it must have been caused by a mine. Moray himself said this, before it occurred to him and his friends that the tale of powder in the Queen's room would be more damaging to her. However, powder stored in the vaulted cellars of the house could have wrecked the building as well as a mine could have done. Besides, if the powder was in the Queen's room and its only purpose the destruction of Darnley, why was the train not fired until 2 a.m.? One account has it that Bothwell's men sat there – with a lighted candle – for hours, and it has been sensibly remarked that if they 'had had any sense they would have lit the fuse and escaped long before; . . . there was no need to tarry'.

The magnitude of the explosion, however, raises questions about the whole scope of the gunpowder plot. That the house should be blown up by a massive explosion simply to kill Darnley reminds one of Charles Lamb's *Dissertation on Roast Pig*. Poison, or a dagger, might surely have disposed of a sick man. The use of powder might have been intended as a demonstration that the murder was no accident or hole-in-the-corner affair, a demonstration made by men who were confident that responsibility would be attributed not to them but to others. But on the face of it the gunpowder plot certainly suggests that the intention was to kill a considerable number of people – Mary and her suite, presumably, as well as, or instead of, the King. There is no difficulty about believing that Mary herself was threatened, as she had been threatened before at the time of Riccio's death, and contemporaries seem to have been quite ready to accept that her life was aimed at. But who wanted the disposal of Mary's train, which almost by definition would itself contain those most likely to aim at her life? Alternatively, if one assumes that the intention was to kill only the King and Queen and their personal attendants, after the nobles had gone away for the night, can we believe that a party of guilty men chatted happily with Mary and Darnley upstairs knowing of the presence of gunpowder in the vaults beneath? It is easier to believe that the large-scale explosion was a mere feint, designed to suggest that Mary and others, as well as Darnley, were the intended victims.

No one has yet discovered exactly what happened at Kirk o'

Field on the morning of 10 February 1567, and no one is now likely to discover it. There were certainly different groups of conspirators. Apart from the fact that, as we have seen, Darnley had made himself personally unpopular, the Riccio murderers, headed by Morton, wanted to kill Darnley purely as an act of personal vengeance. Those who may be called the Protestant politicians, headed by Moray and Maitland, wanted to get rid of Darnley, partly for the honourable reason of freeing the Queen from an intolerable husband but partly to forestall the possible restoration of his influence over the Queen to their own detriment. Bothwell, for his part, wanted to eliminate Darnley to clear the way for his own marriage to the Queen. But, whereas the Riccio murderers and the politicians had nothing to lose should Mary, as well as Darnley, die, Bothwell's interest was different, and if he collaborated with others he may have done so only with the intention of doublecrossing them. If these various parties, with their diverse aims, were not all acting in concert, then the members of one group may have been ignorant of the intentions and actions of others, and this could be one possible explanation of the persistence of mystery. But, however diverse their motives, there is some indication of a plan in which they themselves united but in which different tasks were allotted to different agents.

It is not difficult to determine who in fact are most likely to have been involved in such a co-operative venture. Many fingers were pointed at Sir James Balfour, an able lawyer who had at one time been a close associate of the Protestants but had separated from them on the ground that he was a Lutheran who could not accept the Calvinist theory of the sacrament predominant in Scotland. Balfour had been one of Mary's non-aristocratic familiars in the period after the Chaseabout Raid, and may have had some loyalty to her, but he was so unscrupulous by repute that he could have been associated with any group. His brother, as it happened, had recently received a gift of the provostry of Kirk o' Field, which gave him possession of the new Provost's Lodging, adjoining the fatal house where Darnley lay, and it may have been Sir James who proposed Kirk o' Field

VII Lord Darnley, Mary's second husband

VIII The Earl of Bothwell, Mary's third husband

IX Elizabeth, Queen of England – miniature by Hilliard

X Mary, Queen of Scots – miniature by Hilliard

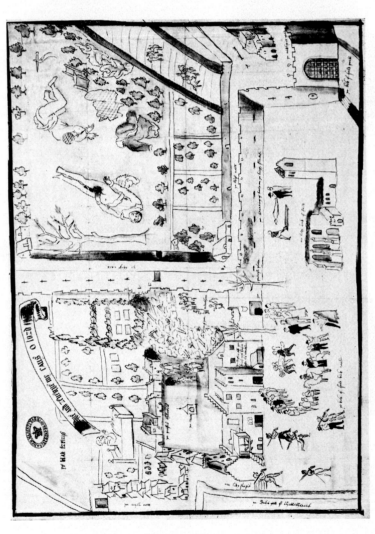

XI   The scene at Kirk o' Field after Darnley's murder – a contemporary sketch

as Darnley's residence. Besides, Balfour was reported to have bought £60 worth of gunpowder shortly before the murder. But Balfour, however deeply he was implicated, was clearly an agent, not a principal.

The record of the Earl of Moray gave much ground for suspicion, and contemporaries saw his hand in the crime. He was an adept at covering his tracks, and, just as he had been ready to enter Edinburgh on the day after Riccio was murdered, so he now left Edinburgh on the day before Darnley was killed, admittedly because his wife had had a miscarriage. In view of his record, his absence was perhaps more suspicious than his presence would have been. He left Scotland early in April, and his decision to go sightseeing abroad at this point suggests that he had had a hand in what had happened and did not want to be involved in the sequel, but to return at a later and appropriate moment with apparently clean hands. He was, in the end, the chief beneficiary of Darnley's murder and what followed from it.

If Moray was conspicuous by his absence, Bothwell was, if some acounts are to believed, conspicuous by his presence. According to the confessions of four of his retainers, a quantity of powder was delivered at his lodging in Holyrood and then conveyed to Kirk o' Field on a pack-horse by some of his men, who bought candles on the way and borrowed a piece of match from some soldiers. The plan had been to put the powder into a barrel and then place the barrel in the Queen's room, but when it was found that the barrel would not go through the doorway the powder was put in bags to be carried in and emptied in a heap on the floor. All this commotion was going on while Mary and her courtiers were with Darnley in the upper storey of the house and presumably passing and re-passing on the stairs. When all was ready, the story goes on, 'French' Paris, one of Bothwell's men, reported to his master in the King's room and Mary's party prepared to leave. As Mary, on her way out, passed Paris, fresh from handling the powder, she remarked, 'Jesu! Paris, how begrimed you are', but she did not pause to inspect her bedroom and returned to Holyrood with Bothwell, whose men remained with the powder and the candles. After midnight Bothwell returned to Kirk o' Field with some of his retainers, answering sentries who challenged them that they were 'My Lord Bothwell's friends'. As Bothwell had doubts about the fuse, he made sure that it was burning and then left the vicinity of the house just before the explosion took place. On the way back to Holyrood his party was again challenged by sentinels, and again proclaimed their identity. This tale contains improbabilities beyond belief, unless Bothwell was an amateurish bungler who sought publicity, but it is hard to credit that it is all pure invention, and the conclusion must be that Bothwell was involved at Kirk o' Field.

The Hamiltons had been in the habit of playing their own hand, and may seem unlikely candidates for collaborating with a diversified group of conspirators. Yet they had joined with Moray when he made his demonstration against the Darnley marriage – the rebellion of 1565 – and if they had the opportunity to take part now in a plot against the heir of their dynastic rivals, the house of Lennox, they would be unlikely to decline it. If they had thus a motive, they also had an opportunity, for Châtelherault, their head, had a house on the north side of the Kirk o' Field quadrangle. The duke himself was in France, but his brother, the Archbishop of St Andrews, was in the house at Kirk o' Field at the time of the murder and there is a tale about a light in one of the windows which was extinguished when the explosion took place. Buchanan, for what his testimony is worth, says that the archbishop conspired with Bothwell to bring Darnley to Kirk o' Field and took up residence there to gloat over the destruction of the King. The prelate is represented as envisaging the destruction of Darnley, the disposal by Bothwell of the young prince, and the ultimate elevation to the throne of the lunatic Earl of Arran, to whom the archbishop would act as curator.

Huntly, too, was at Kirk o' Field, along with his brother-in-law Bothwell on one of his visits. Argyll and Maitland of Lethington were in Edinburgh, and Argyll probably in Mary's company at Kirk o' Field earlier in the evening, but the likelihood is that they were both at Holyrood when Darnley met his death. Morton was not at Kirk o' Field, but, although he stressed in his confession that he had not 'art and part' in the crime, he admitted that he had foreknowledge of it. His kinsman, Archibald Douglas, was at Kirk o' Field, and the presumption is that Archibald was at the head of the band who actually slew Darnley. The dying King, who was the son of Margaret Douglas, was heard to exclaim, 'Pity me, kinsmen, for the sake of Him who had pity on all the world.' This evidence, which rings true, extinguishes the possibility that Darnley, alarmed by the smell from the fuse, rose from his bed and was out of the house before the explosion occurred but was then suffocated by the smoke.

Although these individuals and groups may have been fellow-conspirators, it does not follow that they were all of one mind: some may have intended to kill Mary, others perhaps to kill some of their fellow conspirators. The chance to kill Mary vanished when she left Kirk o' Field, and the delay until 2 a.m. might then be explained by discussions as to whether the explosion should still take place, though now with Darnley alone as a victim. One reporter said that Secretary Maitland had been instrumental in making sure that Mary was reminded of her promise to return to Holyrood, and so saving her life, which other conspirators would have destroyed.

Buchanan said that Archbishop Hamilton sent 'four of his familiar servants to the execution of the murder', and one of Bothwell's retainers said that the leading conspirators had each undertaken to provide two men to take a direct part in executing a jointly agreed plan. Something like this, with the various tasks perhaps determined by lot, seems a probable enough procedure. Thus Bothwell may have provided men to move the powder, though perhaps not from Holyrood or in a barrel, but it is more likely that the prime task of his contingent was to fire the train. The powder is more likely to have been introduced by others, under the immediate direction of Sir James Balfour. If it was stored in an adjoining building and transferred through communicating vaults shortly before the explosion this would help to explain the delay until 2 a.m. and the readiness of the nobles to risk their lives in Darnley's room earlier in the evening. The part of the Douglases was clearly to surround the house to ensure that Darnley did not escape, and it was they who happened to meet the fleeing King, whom they smothered in the garden. It is worth remembering that Moray, in the early days before he decided to pin the crime on his sister, said that more than thirty or forty persons altogether had been involved, and two women who lived nearby gave evidence that they had seen a dozen men leaving the scene after the explosion. There was a concerted effort.

Even if the principals were acting in concert, however, among the subordinates charged with the execution of the scheme there may have been none who knew in full the plans of their masters. One of Bothwell's men said that he saw none besides his own group, 'nor knew of no other companies', and added: 'He knows not but that he [Darnley] was blown in the air; for he [Darnley] was handled by no men's hands, as he saw; and if he was, it was with others and not with them [i.e. his own party].' This speaks of some honest bewilderment, and it can hardly have been lessened when, some days after the crime, Bothwell asked one of his men, 'What thought you when you saw him blown in the air?' Whether we suppose that the principals were acting in concert or that they were participants in a co-operative effort but did not disclose the whole scheme to their subordinates, we can believe that the reason why the truth continues to elude historians may be that it eluded many contemporaries. Those who blew up the house may have believed that they were blowing up the King with it; those who killed him in the garden may have been taken by surprise when the house blew up.

There is, however, the theory that the main plot was one, to which Darnley was privy, against Mary. It is quite likely that Darnley meditated a revolution which would bring about at least the imprisonment of Mary and the coronation of his son, with himself as regent, and – bearing in mind that he had taken part in the Riccio murder, with its threat to Mary – not impossible that he could have thought of a scheme to get rid of his wife and her advisers at one stroke, by a great explosion. He had been prepared to pose as a champion of the papal cause, showing an unwonted devotion to the Mass, and he appealed to the Pope and to Philip of Spain for support on the ground that Mary's policy had been disappointing to zealous Roman Catholics. But, however ostentatious Darnley had been in his devotion to the Mass in recent months, his earlier record was so equivocal that it is hard to believe that even the most optimistic would have thought him a more effective instrument of the Counter-Reformation than Mary, who had in the previous year sent an envoy to the Pope reaffirming her 'constancy towards the Catholic religion and the obedience of the apostolic see', and in December staged a Roman Catholic baptism for her son. Roman Catholic reports of Mary had in fact been highly favourable: she was 'much beloved, esteemed, and honoured', and she was 'most virtuous and religious'; whereas no Roman Catholic agent had much good to say of Darnley.

There is no positive evidence of a Darnley-papalist plot, or even that there was time for any effective co-operation between Darnley and continental powers, and it is easier to believe that various hare-brained schemes merely flitted through the young man's inconstant mind. Besides, there is the difficulty of accepting that a convalescent, from his sick-bed, concocted a large-scale gunpowder plot in the ten days between his arrival in Edinburgh and his death. He could have made no plans in advance, for he did not know that he was going to the old Provost's Lodging, and once he was installed there such supporters as he may have had could have little freedom of action, when Mary and her courtiers – and those who were plotting against him – were constantly passing to and from Kirk o' Field. No contemporary suggested a plot by Darnley, and it does seem odd that if this was indeed the truth the idea did not occur to anyone until nearly four centuries later. And if Darnley had no foreign help it is not too easy to believe that he found accomplices in Scotland itself. Not only was he notorious for his inability to keep secrets, but his betrayal of his fellow-conspirators after the Riccio murder was hardly encouraging to potential allies now. There is in fact less cogent and direct evidence in favour of a gunpowder plot by Darnley than for almost any other theory.

The strength of this theory does, however, lie in the explanation it offers of some details which are otherwise mysterious. If Darnley's agents had planted the powder, then he might have awakened to the smell of burning, perhaps from an accidental fire. It appears, incidentally, that one of his servants, Sandy Durham, had just been dismissed because he had set his bed alight, and the one thing Darnley would be mortally afraid of was fire. He therefore jumped from his bed and fled for his life, only to meet his death – from assassins who happened to be in the garden. Such a headlong flight would explain why Darnley's body was almost naked, while his valet, who would know only of an ordinary fire and saw no need for extreme haste, tarried to bring additional clothing for himself and his distracted master. On the other hand, the hasty exit might perhaps have been the result merely of hearing armed men moving in or around the house. The one theory that is unacceptable is that Darnley himself lit the fuse and then coolly left the house according to a prearranged plan. This requires the belief that he expected Mary and her retinue to return from Holyrood later in the night and that when he saw the torches of a band of men – in reality intending assassins – he mistook them for Mary's company and fired the powder. This left far too much to chance. If the fuse should prove reliable, it might well produce an explosion too soon, especially as there might be some unpredictable last-minute delay before Mary entered the house. But contemporaries had little faith in their fuses, and if there should after all be no explosion, Darnley would have been left with a lot to explain. Besides, if he did fire the fuse, or supervise its firing, why did he return to his bedroom and let himself out of a window, as he seems to have done, and, above all, why did he depart unclothed at 2 a.m. on a February morning? It is true that he had arranged for an early departure, as his horses were ordered for 5 a.m., but something had clearly gone awry. All the circumstances indicate surprise and haste, rather than a pre-arranged exit.

To Mary, the death of Darnley brought something like a breakdown. All the letters sent in her name for a considerable period after the murder, save one on 16 February, are in Scots, not in the French she used for her own letters, and this suggests that she was not taking any personal part in business. On the advice of her council, she went to Seton on 16 February for health reasons, but her activities on the golf links there did not bring about a recovery. So late as 8 March, nearly a month after the crime, an English envoy had an audience in a darkened room in circumstances which strongly suggest that she was unfit to receive him and was impersonated by one of her ladies. Even on 29 March it was reported that she had 'been for the most part either melancholy or sickly' ever since the murder. This breakdown suggests something more than the effect of the death of a husband she did not love, or even of a danger which she herself had escaped. It is possible that the breakdown could have been the result of the tension she had experienced as a guilty plotter against her husband, but it is on the whole un-likely that the successful attainment of her objective would have brought about such complete collapse. It makes better sense to believe that she had been looking forward to a resump-tion of marital relations with her husband as a precaution against disgrace and that his death, on the very night before she was going to sleep with him again, was a disaster. Her collapse would be all the more complete if she reflected that at an earlier stage she herself had encouraged, or at least not discouraged, plots against her husband.

Whatever the truth, and whatever Mary thought, the removal of Darnley seemed so manifestly to her advantage that accusing fingers were soon pointed at her as well as at Bothwell. Cartoons and placards alluding to their guilt began to appear in Edin-burgh less than a week after the murder. It is true that the charges may have been to some extent inspired by those who wanted to discredit her and who had perhaps designed the crime partly to that end. Yet it was not only Protestant Scots, but continental Roman Catholics, who spread the suspicions: the Spanish ambassador in Paris reported that Mary got rid of Darnley, though he added that otherwise Darnley would have killed her, and the Savoyard who had recently been ambassador in Scotland had little doubt that Mary was an accessory to the murder.

The next rumours, inevitably, were that the Queen would marry Bothwell. Despite the lack of evidence of an illicit connection between them before the murder, the readiness now of contemporaries to foresee their marriage is highly suspicious. Already before the end of March there was talk that Bothwell was seeking a divorce, a report that he would marry the Queen had reached Berwick, and in Paris it was being said that Lady Bothwell had been poisoned by her husband to open the way for his marriage to the Queen. A placard set up in Edinburgh on 13 April proclaimed that Bothwell had murdered the husband of the woman he intended to marry and had had her promise long before the murder. By 3 May it was said by an English ambassador in Paris that Mary had arranged the murder so that she could marry Bothwell. It may well be that Mary was not for some time aware of Bothwell's part in the murder. If she wanted to preserve Darnley, Bothwell could hardly have disclosed his contrary intentions. It is true that, if Mary was pregnant, Darnley's death left her, in her desperation, with no alternative to an early marriage to Bothwell, whether or not she knew he was the murderer. Yet on the whole the likelihood is that Bothwell did not reveal his part until he was safely married. He could, of course, have told Mary with perfect truth that he had not killed Darnley. He might subsequently have admitted that he fired the fuse and by doing so had driven Darnley into the hands of his assassins.

Much – perhaps too much – of the discussion of Mary's guilt or innocence has turned on the Casket Letters, any discussion of which must, in the absence of the originals, be inconclusive, for it is impossible to prove the letters either genuine or forgeries. It is also a somewhat barren discussion, for there are indications in plenty that Mary's enemies were unscrupulous enough to produce false evidence against her, and felt it necessary to do so; on the other hand, even if the letters could be shown to be complete fabrications Mary's innocence would not thereby be demonstrated, for the circumstantial evidence against her, not indeed as an accomplice at Kirk o' Field, but as a party to plots against her husband, is overwhelming. The examination and re-examination which the text of the letters has undergone on the whole incline one to the view that they were not indeed forged, but were manipulated.

The contents of the Casket – eight letters alleged to be from Mary to Bothwell, 158 lines of verse, and two contracts for the marriage of Mary and Bothwell – present the following picture if they are read in the sense in which Mary's accusers intended them to be read. Bothwell had ravished her before he won her love, but already while her husband lived she was passionately and devotedly in love with him and was his obedient agent. She arranged to bring Darnley from Glasgow to Craigmillar, and was a party to a plot to dispose of him by violence, for she wrote: 'Think also if you will not find some invention more secret by physic, for he is to take physic at Craigmillar.' In dealing with him in Glasgow she was playing a hypocritical part. Her real feelings were expressed thus: 'Cursed by this pocky fellow that troubleth me thus much . . . I thought I should have been killed with his breath.' Yet she set herself to regain his affection, so that he begged that they should be 'at bed and board together as husband and wife' and she prevailed on him to come to Edinburgh by promising that she would yield to his desires after he was 'purged' or declared free of infection. She formally contracted herself in marriage to Bothwell by 5 April, before he was acquitted and before he was divorced.

There is no real proof of the circumstances of the finding of the Casket, which was said to have been taken from a servant of Bothwell after he had removed it from Edinburgh Castle. There are certainly references, fairly soon after the supposed date of the discovery – 20 June – to the finding of a box containing some papers, but it is far from clear that the alleged contents were identical with those later produced. It is curious, to say the least, that at the end of July Moray and Lennox described a letter which bears some resemblance to 'the Long Glasgow letter' of the Casket but differs from it in important particulars. This version said that Mary agreed to fetch Darnley from Glasgow and would stop at a house on the way to Edinburgh and try to give him a 'draught', which failing she was to put him in the house where the explosion was arranged. This is much more direct than the version ultimately produced, and had it existed it would not have been suppressed; the conclusion seems inescapable that Moray was referring to an early essay at a forgery which was subsequently laid aside in favour of a more subtle concoction which was partly genuine. It is also evident that the contents of the Casket were not at first thought to be as damning as they were subsequently held to be, for on 30 June and 11 July – ten days and three weeks after the discovery of the Casket – the lords were still accusing Bothwell of taking the Queen by force, while the Casket Letters proved that she was his accomplice. It seems beyond doubt that there was a period when the Casket was not considered of any importance, then a period when the potential of tampering with its contents was being considered in various ways, all before the final version took shape. It was only in December that the privy council and the parliament formally declared that Mary's own letters proved her guilt, and even then there was ambiguity, for whereas the privy council referred to letters 'written and subscribed with her own hand' the parliament spoke only of letters 'written wholly with her own hand'. Even after this, the process of adaptation seems to have gone on, for when the papers were first described to the English commissioners at York mention was made of two items which were not produced later – a letter in which Mary stated she had brought about a quarrel between Darnley and her half-brother Lord Robert, and a warrant by Mary authorizing her nobles to sign a bond urging her to marry Bothwell.

The case which has been made out for an amalgam of letters, some by Mary to Bothwell, some by Mary but not to Bothwell, some to Bothwell but not by Mary, with judicious tampering here and there, is convincing. Some of the phraseology, for example about leaving her own country and kinsfolk for her lover's sake, makes nonsense if written by Mary but good enough sense if written by Anna Throndsen, a Norwegian girl to whom Bothwell was betrothed, if not married, but whom he abandoned, or by a Frenchwoman whom he brought to Scotland with him in March 1563 and subsequently neglected. There was no difficulty about copying either genuine letters by other women or interpolated material, in a hand which could easily be mistaken for Mary's, for she wrote a commonplace italic singularly easy to counterfeit. The later use of the letters suggests that Mary's enemies themselves lacked confidence in them. It has been remarked that 'any entirely candid and cautious inquirer . . . will hold . . . that the contents of Morton's casket have been insufficiently authenticated and that Mary must be condemned, if condemned at all, upon other evidence.'

Whatever the truth about the Casket in particular, the question of Mary's complicity in the murder of Darnley has itself been to some extent irrelevant. The action which was fatal to her reputation in the eyes of contemporaries and which cost her her throne was not the murder of Darnley but the marriage to Bothwell. The marriage may well have been, as already suggested, a matter of necessity. Yet there were certain indispensable preliminaries: apart from the not unimportant fact that Bothwell was a married man, he could hardly be married to the Queen before being acquitted of the murder of the late king. On 28 March the privy council fixed his trial for 12 April, but threw the onus of prosecution on to Lennox, the late king's father, instead of on to the Crown, and on the day appointed for the trial Edinburgh was so packed with Bothwell's men that Lennox could not safely appear, with the result that Bothwell was acquitted. Mary had next to make a bid for support, and this she did when parliament met in April. Continuing the policy of appeasement of the reformed Church which she had initiated by financial concessions at the end of 1566, she now took it formally under her protection. The estates also ratified gifts to Morton, Moray, Maitland of Lethington, Huntly, and

Lord Robert Stewart, as well as to Bothwell. Bothwell, on his side, was also playing for support, and this was forthcoming on 19 April in a startling shape: in a formal bond, eight bishops, ten earls, and eleven lords, representing the widest possible range of opinion, pledged themselves to further his candidature for the Queen's hand. Some of them subsequently pleaded that they had agreed to sign only because Bothwell had surrounded Ainslie's Tavern, where they had met for supper, with two hundred hagbutters, and because Bothwell produced the Queen's warrant authorizing them to sign; but, while some of them may have seen the proposed marriage as a means of bringing both Bothwell and the Queen to destruction, others may have been genuinely convinced that Bothwell was the strong man who could restore stability in the realm.

Five days later the strong man showed some of his quality by seizing the Queen as she journeyed from Stirling to Edinburgh and carrying her off to Dunbar. The great difficulty about believing that the abduction was genuine is that after her marriage Mary had at least one opportunity to escape from Bothwell and did not take it: when he had at one stage to leave her in Borthwick Castle, the lords who had risen in arms against them asked her to assist them against her husband's murderer, but she refused. She may not have said, as she was alleged to have done, that 'she cares not to lose France, England, and her own country for him, and shall go with him to the world's end in a white petticoat ere she leaves him', but in later years she does not seem to have been able to make up her mind whether or not she had been forced into the marriage, for sometimes she told one story, sometimes another.

Bothwell, of course, was quite capable of a genuine abduction, and was said to have boasted that he would marry the Queen whether she would or not. If the abduction was genuine, then, followed as it was by a week in Dunbar with Bothwell, it has been argued that after that Mary had no choice but to marry him. It is hard to see clear logic behind it all. A faked abduction could have been a concession to respectability on Mary's part, for she did say that she had turned down his suit

for her hand. But from the point of view of both Mary and
Bothwell the abduction, whether real or pretended, was impolitic, for it simply invited a movement to 'liberate' the Queen.
It may also be asked why, if the Ainslie's Tavern Bond had been
genuine, either Bothwell or Mary thought an abduction necessary. At any rate, contemporaries almost universally regarded
the seizure of Mary's person as a pretence, and condemned her.

The next step was a divorce: on 3 May, in the new commissary court of Edinburgh, the countess obtained a sentence
against her husband, on the ground of his adultery with her
sewing-maid; and on 7 May the earl procured from the court of
the Archbishop of St Andrews a decree that his marriage had
been null for lack of a dispensation. There is another curiosity
here, for a dispensation had in fact been granted by the archbishop himself, and is still extant; but the archbishop, John
Hamilton, may have been a willing party to its suppression in
1567, for its production later would enable the Hamiltons to
bastardize any issue of Mary and Bothwell. It is, indeed, something of a mystery why the dispensation had ever been obtained,
for Bothwell was a Protestant and Huntly, his wife's brother,
was not a zealous Roman Catholic; one wonders whether it was
the bride – who was to show herself a masterly woman throughout – who insisted on leaving nothing to chance.

Bothwell was created Duke of Orkney on 12 May and on 15
May Mary married him at Holyrood. Not many of those who
had signed the bond in his favour were there, and the small
group of notables who did turn up were nearly all on the conservative side in religion. On the very day of the marriage,
Mary wrote to the Pope professing herself his 'most devoted
daughter', but the ceremony was according to the reformed
rite and was conducted by the Protestant Bishop of Orkney.
This may be a measure of Mary's desperation, but, if so, it is
also a measure of her guilt. At the best, she certainly must have
known that Bothwell had had a dispensation for his previous
marriage and that it had been suppressed when he sought a
divorce. But in any event it is not easy to see innocence in a
woman who had chosen Holy Week to make a gift of ecclesias·

tical vestments to a man not yet acquitted of the charge of murdering her husband. The Pope declared on 2 July that it was not his intention to have any further communication with Mary 'unless in times to come he shall see some better sign of her life and religion than he has witnessed in the past', and it has been remarked that 'all her censors agree . . . that Mary's marriage with Bothwell admits of no defence, that it was a shame and a disgrace.' Despite her attempts at the time to defend her marriage in foreign parts, it was a long time before Philip of Spain in particular was prepared to countenance a woman who had gone through a form of marriage with a divorced Pro- testant.

Mary had thrown away her reputation, shown her approval (if nothing more) of her husband's murder, and abandoned the church of her fathers. Yet the marriage, for which she had sacrificed honour and reputation, seems to have brought her no happiness. Even before the marriage ceremony there had been half a day of 'great unkindness' between the pair, and during the honeymoon Mary was heard to ask for 'a knife to stick herself, or else, said she, "I shall drown myself." ' Here is a further mystery which needs explanation. On the barely pos- sible assumption that their relations had been innocent before the marriage, or that Mary had married Bothwell either under compulsion or for purely political reasons, the explanation might simply be that she found him unendurable as a husband. It is not easy to believe that the trouble arose from his infidelity, his jealousy, or his coarse talk, for of these Mary must surely have been aware already. If, of course, it was only after the marriage that Bothwell revealed to her his part in Darnley's murder, that might account for her misery, but on the whole the most reasonable explanation is that Bothwell made some other disclosure which shocked her. Was it something about her mother? It has been suggested that Bothwell's reported remark that 'the Queen' had been 'the cardinal's whore' referred to the relations of Mary of Guise with David Beaton and not to those of Mary herself with one of her Cardinal uncles. Or was it some- thing about Mary's own birth? Scandalous relations between

Bothwell's father and Mary's mother would seem to have been the only possible foundation for the remark 'Some say that he [Bothwell] is near sybbe [closely related] unto Her Grace.'

Bothwell had played for his own hand and had few reliable supporters, while opinion generally was temporarily alienated from a queen who had disgraced herself. Opposition was already being organized before the marriage had taken place, for on 1 May a bond was prepared pledging the signatories to liberate the Queen from Bothwell and to defend her and the prince. Once the marriage had taken place, the proclaimed purpose of the confederate lords was to dissolve it, but some thought that from the outset the real aim was to set up James as King. The design undoubtedly was to transfer power to the Protestant politicians, whether or not with Mary still on the throne. When the opposition assembled in arms, Mary and Bothwell left Holyrood for Borthwick, but they were surprised there; Bothwell made a hurried flight to Dunbar and Mary followed a day or two later, disguised in man's clothing. They hastily raised an army, largely from Bothwell's kinsmen and dependents in East Lothian, but they had the support of few nobles: Huntly and Crawford had been the only earls to appear at council meetings after the marriage. On 15 June the two forces confronted each other at Carberry. There were negotiations over a proposal for a single combat between Bothwell and a champion of the confederates, and in the course of them Mary's army began to melt away. Finally, left with no other choice, the Queen saw Bothwell safely off the field and then surrendered, to be brought to Edinburgh in disgrace – worn out and travel-stained, unsuitably clad, and for the time being broken in spirit to the point of distraction – to be insulted by the crowds. She was sent next day to Lochleven, where on 24 July she was constrained to abdicate in favour of her son and to nominate as regent the Earl of Moray, whom failing, Morton. She well knew that an extorted abdication had no validity. King James VI was crowned at Stirling on 29 July; Knox preached the sermon, but his objections to unction were overruled and the King was crowned and anointed by Adam Bothwell, the Protestant Bishop of Orkney. Moray, who had left for the Continent two days before Bothwell's trial in April, returned on 11 August. He had an interview with his sister in which he obtained a 'voluntary' ratification of her abdication and his nomination as Regent. He was proclaimed Regent on 22 August.

XII   Hermitage Castle

XIII   Lochleven Castle

XIV Mary's execution – an impression by an unknown Dutch artist

5   The Queen's Party 1568-73

The sudden revolution in 1567, and the ease with which Mary was overthrown, probably did not reflect the real state of opinion in the country. What happened was that one section of the insurgents, but only a section, diverted the rebellion into channels of their own choice. When the lords took up arms, their professed purpose had been to punish the murderers of Darnley, to preserve the person of the prince, and to deliver the Queen from 'bondage and captivity'. But within forty-eight hours of her surrender at Carberry she was in genuine bondage and captivity in the island castle of Lochleven, in the custody of Sir William Douglas and his mother, who was the mother also of the Earl of Moray. There may well have been a case for Mary's temporary confinement, because her captors, who must have recalled how she had slipped through their fingers after the murder of Riccio, now found – or professed to find – that she reaffirmed her fidelity to Bothwell, who was still at large and might raise another army. But Bothwell presently withdrew northwards to his dukedom of Orkney. He was then driven from Shetland to Norway, where he was unlucky enough to fall into the hands of the kinsfolk of the Norwegian girl he had seduced and – after some bluster about being King Consort of Scotland – was thrown into prison. The case for Mary's detention became steadily weaker, and the further actions of the confederate lords did not enjoy a great deal of support.

The revolution of 1567 was, we must remember, something unprecedented in the history of the Scottish monarchy. The mere fact of successful rebellion was in itself unusual enough, but the actual deposition of a sovereign by subjects had not been paralleled since the time of remote antiquity, if then. It is true that James III had been overthrown at Sauchieburn in 1488, but he conveniently 'happinit to be slane' immediately afterwards, so that the question of superseding a living sovereign by the heir did not arise. It was something new for a faction to imprison their monarch, extort an abdication, and crown a new king. Opinion must have been in a shocked and puzzled state, and it is no wonder that, while there had been massive support for a rising designed to 'liberate' Mary from Bothwell, there was far more hesitation about the transference of authority from the lawful sovereign. When Moray returned, to assume the regency, his rigorous dealings with his sister did nothing to commend him to moderate men, and his attitude of conscious rectitude – upbraiding her 'like a ghostly father' and threatening her with execution for her adultery – came unfittingly from the leader of a party which was relying on men who had themselves been implicated in the murder of Darnley.

Those who had doubts about the extreme policy of the confederates included Maitland of Lethington and Sir William Kirkcaldy of Grange, who were of the opinion that what Mary had conceded under duress could not prejudice her. Kirkcaldy, an honourable soldier who felt a special responsibility since he had accepted Mary's surrender at Carberry, took the lead in pursuing Bothwell to Orkney and Shetland in an effort to bring him to justice and finally liberate the Queen from him. But, while men like Argyll and Atholl could change sides easily – Argyll deserted the lords a week after Carberry – Kirkcaldy and Maitland did not emerge as open Marians until much later and were at first numbered among 'secret favourers of the Queen'. Thus, while the minority of lords who decided to crown James came to constitute 'the King's Men', those who separated from them joined others who had never been parties to the confederacy and formed the party of 'the Queen's Men'. Huntly and Lord John Hamilton (Châtelherault's second surviving son) had actually been on their way to join Mary when the encounter at Carberry had taken place. The motives of the Hamiltons will be examined later, but it may be said here that they formed the core of the Queen's party.

Moray's position, all in all, was far from secure. Once again, as at the time of the Chaseabout Raid, he had failed to reproduce the circumstances of the successful revolution of 1560, for there was neither unanimity in Scotland nor English support for his party. After Carberry, Elizabeth had sent an envoy to deal for Mary's release on condition that she repudiated Bothwell, and although, when he succeeded in communicating with her at Lochleven, he found that she would not contemplate divorce, Elizabeth still refused to acknowledge Moray's administration as the legal Scottish government. Yet Moray's power was on the whole increasing as long as Mary was in Lochleven, and had she remained there he might have consolidated his position. She was, however, an embarrassing captive: her mere existence was a living challenge to Moray, and very soon, recovering her health and spirits, she set herself to bring her charms to bear on her warders, ultimately with success. At least one attempt to liberate her failed, but ultimately, thanks to the help of Willie Douglas, a young member of the household, she escaped on 2 May 1568. The escape caught Moray at Glasgow, in a district where his opponents were strong, and his force was outnumbered by the army raised for the Queen. Mary's advisers decided to make for the stronghold of Dumbarton, which was held by a friend, Lord Fleming, but her army was outmanoeuvred as it passed Glasgow and was routed at Langside on 13 May. Mary fled, by Sanquhar and Terregles, to Dundrennan, and on 16 May crossed the Solway in a fishing boat to land at Workington in Cumberland. She was received next day by the deputy governor of Carlisle, who conducted her to Cockermouth and then to Carlisle Castle.

All historians are familiar with the Hundred Days of Napoleon, that brief period when, on his return from Elba, he reorganized a government, mustered a great army, and fought at Waterloo an action which his victorious adversary pronounced to have been no foregone conclusion. Such were the Hundred Days of Napoleon. Perhaps equally memorable should be the

Eleven Days of Mary Stewart, the days, that is, between her escape from Lochleven on 2 May 1568 and the battle of Langside on the 13th. Admittedly, provisional arrangements must have been made to receive her should she escape. But no one could count on the success of Willie Douglas and his sleight of hand in lifting the keys of the castle, and it is inconceivable that substantial numbers of men were already standing by, mustered and armed, ready for a contingency which might not arise. A summons, a whole series of summonses, must have gone out with the utmost speed, and they were answered with an alacrity which shows how strong was the support which Mary had.

In her flight, Mary crossed the Firth of Forth and first halted at Niddrie Castle, near Winchburgh, a few miles south-west of Queensferry. Niddrie was a stronghold of Lord Seton, one of her staunchest supporters, and he would presumably at once send out messengers to East Lothian, where his own influence chiefly lay, and to other parts of the south-east. Mary's call at Niddrie probably enabled messages to reach men in the south-east who would otherwise have found it difficult to join her army in time for Langside. At Niddrie Mary spent only two hours, and then rode on to Hamilton. She was already there on the 3rd, the day after her escape, and remained there until the morning of the engagement at Langside, ten miles away. Hamilton must have been the scene of almost incredible activity, directed mainly to raising the centre and the south-west of the country.

The result was that, in her marvellous Eleven Days, Mary seems to have mustered between 5,000 and 6,000 men. The French ambassador, who may be presumed to have had some experience of what mustering an army involved, remarked to Sir James Melville that he 'never did see so many men so suddenly convened'. This remarkable response to the Queen's summons may, it can be suggested, give a truer picture of Scottish opinion than the *coup* of 1567. It is clear that an analysis of the party which fought for Mary at Langside and for years after Langside must yield some indication of the real strength of her cause and some measure of the extent to which she can be reckoned a popular and successful sovereign.

A bond pledging support to the Queen was signed at Hamilton on 8 May by no less than nine earls, nine bishops, seventeen lords, fourteen commendators, and about ninety lairds. This in itself would be remarkable enough, but with that Hamilton Bond we may read a bond drawn up at Dumbarton on 12 September, after Mary had been four months in England and it had become apparent that some kind of inquiry into her alleged crimes was going to be held there. Mary's supporters, gathered at Dumbarton to declare their readiness to arrange for her defence before an English tribunal, numbered only a few less than those who had gathered at Hamilton before Langside: there were seven earls, twelve lords, eight bishops, and nine commendators. This puts it beyond all doubt that Mary's cause, after she had abandoned Scotland and reached England, was by no means that of a friendless refugee. But we have also far more evidence than those two bonds afford, and evidence which gives much information about men of lesser rank as well as about notables. Thanks to the escheats, respites, and remissions recorded in the Register of the Privy Seal, we know the names of something like 500 men of all degrees who fought for Mary at Langside. This means that we have the names of nearly a tenth of her entire army, and enables us to make an analysis with some confidence.

In 1568 there were about nineteen earls on what may be called the active list, though this figure includes Sutherland and Menteith, who were still under twenty, and Montrose, who was nearly eighty. Of the nineteen, eleven or twelve can be put down as committed Marians – a marked contrast to the five earls who are named as being present at the coronation of King James. There is an equally sharp contrast between the seventeen lords who signed the Hamilton Bond and the eight who were at James's coronation. So far as the bishops were concerned, there was something very close to unanimity for the Queen. Of the commendators, fourteen signed the Hamilton Bond on Mary's behalf and the nine who signed the Dumbarton Bond included four who had not been at Hamilton: this means that Mary had the support of more than half of the commendators.

The most telling analysis, Scottish society being what it was, is an analysis by families. Outstanding on the Queen's side were of course the Hamiltons. The head of the house, the second Earl of Arran, better known as the Duke of Châtelherault, had been in exile since the Chaseabout Raid, and did not return to Scotland until February 1569, when he became the figurehead of the Queen's party. His eldest son, the erstwhile suitor of Mary and of Elizabeth, was insane, and his next surviving son, Lord John Hamilton, showed few of the qualities of leadership. But the Hamilton interest was still guided by the two astute ecclesiastics who were kinsmen of the duke – John Hamilton, Archbishop of St Andrews, and Gavin, Commendator of Kilwinning and coadjutor of St Andrews. The cadet branches of the house turned out in force to support its head: among the persons who are known to have been present at Langside there are thirty-eight Hamiltons, twenty-four of them lairds; and of the thirty-four persons named as parties to the Pacification of Perth, which ultimately went a long way to bringing the civil war to an end, no less than twenty-four were Hamiltons.

Some of the other peers who were among the leaders of Mary's party – Fleming, Eglinton, Huntly, and Argyll – were closely related to the Hamiltons by marriage. In general, marriage connections did not prove important as links in sixteenth-century Scottish politics, for the period shows many examples of brothers-in-law, fathers-in-law, and sons-in-law belonging to contrary parties. But in this particular instance marriage connections with the Hamiltons had real importance. This arose from the state of the royal succession and the proximity of the Hamiltons to the Crown. One reason for the Hamilton interest in favour of Mary as opposed to James was the simple fact that, while the Hamiltons were unquestionably heirs presumptive to Mary, it was not so clear that they were heirs presumptive to James if he were recognized as King. James's father, Darnley, had been King, and this raised the question whether the succession to James, if he had no issue, should pass to Darnley's

family, the Lennoxes, who had in any event a secondary claim
to the succession owing to the shadow of doubt which hung
over the legitimacy of Châtelherault. This is no mere matter
of speculation: it was seriously argued by constitutional lawyers at the time. Another matter that was seriously argued was
the right to the regency. While some lawyers thought that the
regency belonged of right to the heir presumptive, others
thought that the selection of a regent was a matter for council
or parliament. The Hamiltons argued that, if Mary were deposed and a regency necessary, it should go to Châtelherault,
as heir presumptive, and there was little hope that they would
be reconciled to Moray.

It is easy to talk of 'the Hamiltons' as heirs to Mary, but what
was the exact state of the succession? Châtelherault's eldest
son was a hopeless imbecile. The next son, Gavin, was already
dead. Lord John, the effective heir, was not yet married, nor
were his younger brothers, David and Claude. It appeared,
therefore, at this stage that the succession might be open to
Châtelherault's daughters and their descendants. One daughter,
Barbara, had married Lord Fleming, and had by him a daughter.
The Lord Fleming who was at this stage a member of the Queen's
party was the brother of Barbara's husband, but the marriage
may well have done something to bring him into the Hamilton
nexus. The next daughter, Jean, had married the Earl of Eglinton, and although they had been divorced, Eglinton was in the
Queen's party. Then came Anne, wife of the fifth Earl of
Huntly, one of Mary's strongest supporters and the father of
two sons who, in the event of appropriate casualties, might
well have their prospects. Going a generation further back,
Helen Hamilton, Châtelherault's sister, had married the fourth
Earl of Argyll, and this brought the Argylls into the Hamilton
connection.

There is no need to argue that all those peers were in the
Marian party simply because of their reversionary rights to the
royal succession. But it is hard to be sure how far dreams of a
crown might go. It was reported in 1567 that the Hamiltons,
Argyll, and Huntly were all for Mary on the ground that if

they opposed her and she were nonetheless restored no one stood to lose more than those who were nearest to the Crown. The Hamiltons coolly calculated not only that if Mary lived she might marry either Lord John Hamilton or Argyll's brother, but also that it would be far better for their cause if she were to die: 'For she being taken away, they account but the little King, who may die, between them and *home*.' In short, the Hamiltons were saying 'Get rid of Mary, get rid of James, and then "we are home", that is, on the throne.' If that is how people calculated, there can be little doubt that speculation and aspiration extended far beyond the prospective lives of Mary and James.

The other earls, who were not within the Hamilton nexus, had various reasons for supporting Mary. Cassillis was on the Roman Catholic side in religion, and Crawford's tendencies seem to have been similar. Atholl, although he did not sign either the Hamilton Bond or the Dumbarton Bond, had nevertheless opposed the Protestant legislation in 1560. His wife was a Fleming and, although he had taken part in James's coronation and seems to have been oddly reluctant to come out openly on Mary's side, he could hardly have been other than sympathetic to her cause. On the other hand, Marischal had tended to the Protestant and pro-English side, as had Montrose, but when they joined the Queen's party they were at one with many others who had similar records, and allowance must be made for genuine political convictions. Rothes had an even clearer record, for his family had been strongly Protestant, and his attachment to Mary's cause may have owed something to his feud with Lord Lindsay, who was one of the most bigoted of the King's supporters. Menteith was the son of a zealous Protestant, but his mother was a daughter of Mary's strenuous supporter Lord Seton and we cannot discount possible maternal influence on a man who was still only about nineteen. Caithness and Errol seem to have been previously uncommitted, although they now joined Mary's party. The young Earl of Sutherland is especially interesting. He was himself a Gordon, he was later to marry a Gordon, and it looks as if the Huntly interest or connection would have brought him into Mary's party; but in 1567 the fifteen-year-old youth had been married, more or less by force, to a daughter of the Earl of Caithness, who had acquired wardship over him, and in 1568 he can have had no option but to side with the father-in-law who controlled him.

The handful of earls who were on the King's side are straight-forward cases. Moray was moved primarily by ambition, by a genuine attachment to the Protestantism which he persisted in believing that Mary threatened, and by his feud with Huntly. Morton was following the long-standing tradition of his house, the Angus Douglases, in supporting the Reformation and the English alliance, and of course he had been quite alienated from Mary by his part in the Riccio murder. Glencairn was a bigoted Protestant. Lennox, as Darnley's father and the King's grand-father, had his personal and dynastic motives as well as his hereditary rivalry with Mary's supporters, the Hamiltons. The Earl of Mar had never been a strong party man, but he was the King's guardian and a fundamentally honest man, who saw it as his duty to preserve King James against possible danger from Hamiltons and others.

The bishops, it has been noted, were almost unanimously for the Queen. But this was not because they were all papists, and indeed there were only two or three of them whose choice seems to have been determined by religious considerations. The two intransigent papalists – Beaton of Glasgow and Chisholm of Dunblane – were, appropriately enough, out of the country, and although they were Marians they had no influence to speak of on events in Scotland at this stage. The only bishops in the country who may have been inclined to the Queen primarily by religious convictions were Crichton of Dunkeld, a respectable figure and a fairly consistent conservative, and John Lesley of Ross, though neither of them was anything like an out-and-out papist, and both had their family affiliations with the Queen's side: the Crichtons generally, as we shall see, were for the Queen, and Lesley looked to the Earl of Rothes, a supporter of Mary, as the head of his house. There were other bishops with whom family considerations were plainly paramount. William

Gordon of Aberdeen and Alexander Gordon of Galloway, though one was a conservative and the other a committed Protestant, naturally took the side supported by the Earl of Huntly, head of the house of Gordon. The Archbishop of St Andrews and the Bishop of Argyll were both Hamiltons, and that placed them firmly enough. Hepburn of Moray was the great-uncle of Mary's third husband and was naturally to be found in a party which, as we shall see, had much Hepburn backing. Brechin was a Campbell, and, though not very closely related to the Earl of Argyll, followed his chief. Carswell of the Isles was a protégé of the Argyll family, and it is not difficult to account for his allegiance to Mary on that score, though, to be fair, he may have had a sense of gratitude to the Queen who had given him a bishopric although he was an active Protestant.

Out of the thirteen bishops, only two were on the King's side. Robert Stewart of Caithness, brother of the Earl of Lennox, was uncle of Darnley and great-uncle of the little King, so there could be no doubt where he would stand. The one bishop who remains is Adam Bothwell of Orkney. His family affiliations were partly middle-class, and indeed he was the most middle-class man in the whole hierarchy, but kinship might have been expected to put him on the Queen's side, for he was connected by marriage to Kirkcaldy of Grange and to the Melvilles who were so loyal to Mary. Yet, after officiating at the marriage of Mary to the Earl of Bothwell, he crowned James VI and supported the King's party. If we can allow that two or three of Mary's episcopal supporters had conscientious motives, it may perhaps be permitted to claim similar motives for one of the King's episcopal supporters.

Earls, lords, and bishops did not themselves make a numerically significant contribution to Mary's armies, but each had his following and his influence. It is therefore important to analyse the lesser men. This analysis becomes largely one by geography, though of course territorial and family associations were intertwined. Perhaps the most surprising feature is the number of men from south-eastern Scotland – the region from Midlothian to the eastern Borders – who appear in the Queen's party, sum-

moned, no doubt, by messages sent out during her brief stay at
Niddrie. About 120 men from this area are named as being
present at Langside – roughly a quarter of the total names
known – and another thirty or so appear in the roll of the
Queen's Men in some other capacity. When we recall that the
south-east had been one of the most Protestant and pro-English
parts of Scotland, this is very remarkable. We find the very
men appearing among the Queen's supporters now who had
appeared again and again in earlier years as supporters of the
Reformation and of the English: men like Broun of Colstoun,
Wauchope of Caikmure, Hepburn of Waughton, Fawside of
that ilk, Cranston of Thirlestane Mains, Heriot of Trabroun,
and a host of others, whose names are familiar to students of
the period as reformers and anglophiles. Why were they in
Mary's party? Leaving aside the imponderable elements of conscience and political principles, we must ask what families had
the chief influence in that area.

In the first place, there was Hepburn influence. Bothwell himself, though he may not have been a good Christian, was a firm
Protestant, and he had always carried with him a good many of
the godly lairds of the south-east, the natural dependants of the
Lord of Hailes, Crichton, and Dunbar. Among the Queen's supporters at Langside were no less than eight Hepburn lairds, and
it is hard to say how many more may have been Hepburn dependants. It was a continuation of the support Bothwell had had at
Carberry, where the lairds of Langton, Waughton, Wedderburn,
and Bass had been with him, and both Bass and Waughton, at
least, were again in the Queen's army at Langside. Secondly,
next to Hepburn influence, there was the influence of Lord
Seton. Twenty-five of his dependants are mentioned in a single
document as supporters of Mary, mostly men from Tranent,
Preston, Winton, and Longniddry. Thirdly, and perhaps more
mysteriously, there was the interest of Sir William Sinclair of
Roslin. Of him and his opinions and motives there seems to be
little information, though it may have counted with him that
the Earl of Caithness, head of his house, was on Mary's side.
At any rate, Sir William was himself in the Queen's army at

Langside, and twenty-two of his dependants are also named as being there. Fourthly there was Lord Hay of Yester, who signed both the Hamilton and Dumbarton bonds. These four – Hepburn, Seton, Sinclair, and Hay – were the main influences, but one can see other examples of family cohesion. For example, Lauder of Bass was not the only Lauder in the Queen's army at Langside. Again, Lord Borthwick was at Langside, and a number of other Borthwicks were in the Queen's army. Further to the south-east, although Lord Home ultimately joined the Queen's party, he seems to have been a latecomer, for he did not sign either the Hamilton or the Dumbarton bond, and only a single member of his family is recorded as present at Langside. Ker of Fairnihirst, a Borderer, was, like Home, a leading Marian later on. Of course, Berwickshire and the Borders are further away from Niddrie or Hamilton, and the time factor may account for the lack of support from that area for Mary at Langside.

The other main recruiting ground for the Langside campaign – for geographical reasons the most important of all – was the south-west, that is, the whole region from West Lothian to Dumfriesshire. As against 120 men from the south-east, one can count no less than 280 from the south-west as present at Langside, plus a handful who appear as Marians in some other capacity. If the proportion of the names we have to the total number of men in the Queen's army at Langside is anything like constant – that is, about a tenth – then it looks as if about half of Mary's force came from the south-western region. As most of the summonses had gone out from Hamilton, this is not surprising, and there are not many dynastic surprises either.

There was, in the first place, the Hamilton interest itself, in West Lothian and Lanarkshire. But Mary had other supporters in the south-west besides Hamilton. Lord Fleming had his following, as had Lord Boyd: no less than thirty Boyds are mentioned by name. There was a very good turnout of Crawfords – twenty-eight of them named – no doubt mainly from Lanarkshire, but there is no indication whose influence swayed them. The Earl of Glencairn no doubt mustered the Cunninghams and other dependants, though only seven Cunninghams are recorded

as among Mary's supporters, and they were scooped up long
after Langside, when Dumbarton Castle fell to the King. Equally,
Eglinton would bring out the Montgomeries, though only six
are named among those present at Langside; and the Kennedies,
whom Cassillis would bring out, are even more poorly represented by name. It has to be remembered that the following of
an earl or a lord consisted very largely of men who did not
bear his surname, so names are only a partial guide. Several
south-western names which were held mainly by men of lairdly
rank figure fairly prominently in the Langside roll – six Baillies,
six Stewarts, eight Barclays, seven Dalziels, half a dozen Wal-
laces. It must always be kept in mind that the figures we have
are out of a total representing only a tenth or less of the Queen's
army, so that even half a dozen names may represent a turnout
of sixty. Lord Maxwell made a fair showing, and it is of interest
to find that, besides Maxwells from their real country in the far
south, the Queen's army at Langside included Maxwells of Pol-
lock, who had the advantage that the battle took place almost
on their doorstep.

There is no doubt about the way the south-west rose for the
Queen, and the motives at work would repay closer analysis. One
attempt has been made to examine a locality in this context,
by Sir James Fergusson in *The White Hind* (1963). He comments
on George Corrie of Kelwood:

Although a neighbour and dependant of the Earl of Cassillis he
himself was an avowed and consistent reformer. Like young Bar-
gany [who fought in Moray's army at Langside], he had subscribed
the Book of Discipline; and he had also signed the Ayr Covenant
of 1562 and the Bond of Association against Popery in 1567.

The inference once more is that political decision or choice of
allegiance in 1568 cut right across ecclesiastical affiliations.
Sir James, in this paper, was writing of the progress Mary had
made through Ayrshire in 1563, and he remarks thoughtfully:

There is no contemporary report of what impression she made
on those who there entertained her, heard her speak and laugh, or
merely watched her ride past. But some evidence that she left them

a lasting and happy memory seems to lie in the striking number of Ayrshiremen who five years later rallied to her standard after she escaped from Lochleven and fought for her at the battle of Langside.

There were at Langside a number of men from Fife, who may well have heard the news from Lochleven itself and not had to wait for a summons from Niddrie or Hamilton. We need not be surprised at the appearance of George Douglas, brother of the laird of Lochleven, for he had himself attempted Mary's rescue earlier and would no doubt be aware of the plan for her ultimate escape. Nor need we be surprised that David Seton of Parbroath supported Lord Seton and brought some of his people with him. There was remarkable support from the Balfours, whose motives it is hard to detect. At Langside there were present Balfour of Pitullo, Balfour of Bandone, Balfour of Nether Gogar, and the son of Balfour of Inchery. Balfour of Pittendreich became a Marian, though he was not at Langside, and the same is true of George Balfour, Commendator of the Charterhouse, as well as of Gilbert Balfour of Westray, although his properties and interests lay in far-away Orkney. If the Balfours' motives are inexplicable, they certainly showed cohesion. Among other Fife men, Leslie of Parkhill naturally followed Leslie, Earl of Rothes. Yet more Fifers joined the Queen's party later – the loyal Melvilles among them: Robert Melville of Cairny and two of his brothers, as well as their brother-in-law Kirkcaldy of Grange. Once again, it is to be observed in Fife as in East Lothian that many lairds turn up on the Queen's side who had good records as Protestants. The same applies to a couple of lairds from nearby Clackmannanshire – Blackadder of Tullyallan and Bruce of Clackmannan.

There is a sharp contrast when we turn from the south of the country to the north. There was hardly anyone in Mary's army from north of the Tay, where, it may be presumed, there was strong support for her cause and whence thousands might have come flocking had time allowed. In the hurried days of organization at Hamilton, there was little hope of getting messages in time to people north of the Tay. Consequently, it is not surprising that no one from Angus is mentioned as being in the Queen's army, though a number of Angus families – Ogilvies and Lindsays, Beatons and Guthries – appear in her party later. Oddly enough, there were four Aberdeenshire men at Langside – a couple of Cheynes, a Gordon, and an Innes. One can only conclude that they happened to be somewhere in the south when the news of the Queen's escape broke and that they hastened to join her army in time. Later on, of course, there was any number of recruits to the Queen's party from Aberdeenshire and further north. There is one rather remarkable list which contains the names of no less than 103 persons who took part with Adam Gordon of Auchindoun in an action against the King's forces at Craibstane in Aberdeenshire in November 1571. They are nearly all from Sutherland, largely Gordons and Murrays, dependants of the Earl of Sutherland, who, as we saw, had been committed to Mary from the outset.

There is one further piece of territorial analysis which requires special attention, namely, the situation in Edinburgh. Among the lists of men present at Langside, there are very few burgesses – one from Glasgow, one from Kilmarnock (both Boyds), and one from Ayr (a Crawford). It may be that the burgesses generally were more opposed to the Queen; it may be that the burgesses were on the whole simply not fighting men. But in Edinburgh, although only three burgesses are named as having been in Mary's army at Langside – one of them a Frenchman and another one of the Queen's own servitors – no less than seventy-four were named later as accessories to Kirkcaldy of Grange when he was holding the castle for the Queen. Now, we know that Kirkcaldy was able to put considerable pressure on the burgesses, and we know that he had to get supplies for his garrison. We can guess, too, that the merchants and craftsmen were not averse from selling their goods and services in a ready market, without regard to politics. It certainly appears that Kirkcaldy and his men were doing themselves fairly well: they had supplies from three apothecaries, three candlemakers, six maltmen, four bakers, nine tailors and clothiers, two goldsmiths, two shoemakers, three skinners, two smiths, and a great many more, including Thomas Bassandyne, who was soon to achieve some note as the printer of the first Bible produced in Scotland. Making all allowances, this information is startling. It has often been said that the aristocratic strength of Mary's party was counterbalanced by middle-class support for the young King and his regents, but it would seem that this has been too sweeping a generalization.

The other group about whom something should be said are the professional men. The impression one forms from an examination of their record is that, if Mary's party had birth and breeding on its side, professional experience on the whole lay with her adversaries. Even the clergy – apart from the bishops and commendators, who were mainly aristocratic and followed the majority of the nobles into Mary's camp – do not figure much in the Marian party. Of sixteen names which come to light, three were Hamiltons, one a Hepburn, one a Campbell, and one a Hume, who obviously went with their families. Besides, among those sixteen, the great majority were dignitaries – five provosts of collegiate churches, the Archdeacon of Ross, and James Thornton, that most notorious of Scottish pluralists, who held a hand-picked bunch of dignities scattered throughout the length and breadth of Scotland. What one might call the rank and file of the clergy are hardly represented at all – a couple of prebendaries of the collegiate church of Yester, presumably following their patron, Lord Hay of Yester, and a vicar who was a Hamilton. Some of the sixteen 'clergy' were really laymen in disguise, although they held benefices, like David Chalmer, Chancellor of Ross, who was better known as David Chalmer of Ormond and a lawyer. Among the whole lot there was only one minister – Thomas Hepburn, parson and minister of Oldhamstocks, who was not only a Hepburn but had been with George Dalgleish, the Earl of Bothwell's servant, when, as it was alleged, he went into Edinburgh Castle to remove the famous Casket. There was also one vicar who was a reader, or assistant minister, in the reformed Church. But before we jump to the conclusion that the Protestant clergy were generally opposed to Mary – though they may have been –

we must remind ourselves that we are relying largely on evidence for the battle of Langside and that not many ministers were likely to appear under arms on either side. At any rate, there are no clear signs of cases of conscience, and while Protestantism may on balance have kept a lot of clergy from supporting the Queen it was not strong enough to keep them out of her party altogether.

The other professional men who counted were lawyers and officials. When Mary's first trial took place in England in 1568, Moray was able to produce a galaxy of talent – a group of lawyers and councillors like Bishop Adam Bothwell, Robert Pitcairn, Commendator of Dunfermline, and Henry Balnaves of Halhill, besides outstanding figures like George Buchanan, Maitland of Lethington, and MacGill of Rankeillor Nether, the Lord Clerk Register. On the other hand, none of Mary's commissioners at that point could be put down as first-raters intellectually, though John Lesley, Bishop of Ross, and Gavin Hamilton, Commendator of Kilwinning, had some professional experience. Yet a fair sprinkling of lawyers were to be found among Mary's supporters – Robert Crichton of Eliok, who had been Lord Advocate and was at Langside, Sir James Balfour of Pittendreich, an ex-Clerk Register, Thomas Makcalyean of Cliftonhall, one or two other advocates like John Moscrop, and the commissary clerk of Dunblane, John Muschet. Subsequently, Maitland of Lethington and his brother John, the future Lord Thirlestane, joined Mary's party. Some of the lawyers were in the Queen's party for family reasons – Crichton and Balfour noticeably. Yet one just wonders whether Mary's predominantly aristocratic party may have failed to realize the support they might derive from professional men, skilfully used, and perhaps rather tended to despise them.

All in all, it is evident that the Queen's party was far stronger than is often believed. The history of those eleven days after the flight from Lochleven is not the least instructive in Mary's whole career. No doubt the pitiable tale of her misfortunes as a woman aroused sympathy, and no doubt some who found that they enjoyed less influence under the new régime than they had expected were now ready to try to overthrow the regency. But that Mary, after the ineptitude, the folly, she had displayed in the last year or two, and after the shame and disgrace she had incurred, could command so much support, would seem to be at once significant of Scottish attachment to the lawful sovereign and creditable to her own record in her earlier years. And one thing that does stand out is that ecclesiastical issues hardly counted: the sooner we rid ourselves of the idea that the revolution of 1567 had anything to do with deposing an idolatrous queen the better, though Mary's enemies tried to push this as a propaganda line. This was seen clearly enough by contemporaries. John Spottiswoode, Superintendent of Lothian, wrote more in sorrow than in anger that

albeit that all the papists within the realm of Scotland had joined with her, the danger had not been great. . . . But alas! . . . to see the hands of such as were esteemed the principal within the flock to arm themselves against God.

Why, then, did the Queen's party fail, and why did the King's party prevail? One possible answer is a fairly simple one. In the first place, Langside should never have been fought at all, and there can be little doubt that if Mary had been able to wait to produce a better organization and to bring in the additional forces which would have come from the north, she could have sweptMoray away in rout. There could have been another Chase-about Raid. The responsibility for the ill-considered engagement was laid at the door of the Hamiltons, who for the time being were the dominant force in Mary's entourage and hoped that a victory would ensure their continued supremacy and make it impossible for Mary to avoid commitment to Lord John. To wait until the northern magnates arrived in force would have weakened their position and made less practicable any nefarious designs they may have had against Mary.

But, after Langside had been fought and lost, Mary's fatal error was to flee the country. It was an impetuous, precipitate decision, not in character with much that she did, and it was the negation of calculated policy. Had she remained in Scotland there is no doubt that she could have been once more at the head of a respectable force, indeed of a larger army than had fought for her at Langside. That battle, though a defeat, did not produce many casualties on either side, and Mary's forces would have rallied again, reinforced by others. Her supporters were certainly intending to continue the war with vigour.

In subsequent years, it was Mary's detention in England – brought on by her own rash decision to flee in 1568 – that was fatal to her chances. However strong her party might be, and however they might succeed in impressing Elizabeth personally, there was probably no real chance that Elizabeth's advisers would ever have consented to Mary's release and return to Scotland on terms which would have satisfied her supporters. Therefore, her cause in Scotland, which might so easily have prevailed in her presence, was lost through her absence. Her party must have begun to wonder, from 1569 onwards, what it was really fighting for, when there was little chance of achieving its original objective of restoring the Queen. The party probably had its maximum strength in 1568. From that point onwards there were more desertions than accessions, and the number of her supporters dwindled for lack of a realistic objective. And the war between the Queen's Men and King's Men does seem to have degenerated into a kind of aimless baronial scrap in which little principle was any longer involved.

6   The First Trial

The first phase of Mary's life in England centred around investigations which dragged on for four months at York, Westminster, and Hampton Court at the end of 1568 and the beginning of 1569. These proceedings may be held to constitute her first trial. In her second and better-known trial, which led to her execution at Fotheringhay in 1587, the crime of which she was accused was complicity in plots against the life of Queen Elizabeth. But when Mary was tried for the first time, in 1568–9, the crime laid to her charge was complicity in the murder of her second husband, and the punishment which she incurred was, in effect, a sentence of life imprisonment.

This phase forms something of a watershed in Mary's biography, between the girl in France and the reigning Queen of Scotland on one side, and, on the other, a prematurely ageing captive and a tragic royal martyr. Both of these come together in the familiar picture of Mary. But the Mary of 1568–9 is in some ways a less attractive and romantic figure: she was then a fugitive from justice as a suspected murderess, her life was in peril from her own subjects, she was bent on vengeance, she was ready to abandon Bothwell for whom she had sacrificed so much, ready too to flirt with Anglicanism as a condition of her restoration. At this stage the situation was fluid and there was a corresponding fluidity in Mary's attitudes. But if her behaviour is to be interpreted as all along dominated mainly by opportunism, there is nothing in her conduct at this stage which is inconsistent with what went before and what followed.

That there should be a trial, an investigation, was by no means a foregone conclusion. The situation which was created by

Mary's arrival in England was startling to a degree which is now hard to appreciate. In the twentieth century we live in a world well stocked with exiled monarchs, and have grown accustomed to England's providing them with homes. But, even had the spectacle of a deposed and refugee crowned head been familiar in the sixteenth century – which it was not – Mary's deposition had not resulted from a political or dynastic revolution: she had lost her throne because she was suspected of murdering her husband and had entered into a scandalous marriage, which were offences in private law rather than in public law. It complicated the matter further that if Mary, the suspect, was a queen, Darnley, the victim, was no less a king and, like herself, of the royal blood of England. No precedent existed for dealing with such a situation.

Mary's flight to England had been a matter of impulse rather than calculation: she was in terror for her life. She did say at one stage that if Elizabeth would not help her she would return to Scotland 'in that same sober boat wherein she came', but this was mere rhetoric. Any calculation which had entered into her decision had been the calculation that she could count on English help, and – unless her friends in Scotland could engineer a counter-revolution in her absence – English help was essential, either to restore her by force or to mediate between her and her subjects. She professed to make much of her hopes in France, and her requests to be allowed to pass through England into France were perhaps a little more serious than her threat to return to Scotland. But her prospects in France were not good. That country had had little respite from civil war, and the direction of affairs was largely in the hands of Catherine de' Medici, who had no more use for Mary now than she had in 1561. At this stage – not inappropriately for 'a merchant's daughter' – Catherine seems to have been more interested in the fate of Mary's pearls than in the fate of her person. France, far from maintaining Mary's right, was showing some disposition to recognize Moray's government. Mary's talk of aid from France was chiefly designed to improve her bargaining position with the English, and it has been suggested that if she had been allowed to go to the Continent she might well have sunk into oblivion as a tiresome and importunate woman, for whom none of the continental powers was likely to have any consistent use and all of whom were more likely to see her as possessing merely a nuisance value against Elizabeth than to try to restore her.

There was, however, a serious dilemma for the English government, and it was analysed almost at once by Mr Secretary Cecil, an indefatigable writer of memoranda in which he coldly summed up the pros and cons of various courses of action. If Mary were allowed to 'pass to France', he thought, the Franco-Scottish alliance against England would be revived. If she were allowed to remain in England, she would be a focus of disaffection against Elizabeth. If she returned to Scotland, the friends of England there would be 'abased' and the friends of France exalted. He summed it up thus: 'We find neither her continuance here good, nor her departing hence quiet for us.' Elizabeth's envoys to Mary remarked that their Queen would be open to criticism if she continued to detain the Scottish Queen and that it was dishonourable to keep her 'so rigorously a prisoner' as she was being kept at Carlisle. It was all very difficult, but Mary could hardly be permitted to range freely through England, and communication with her had to be established while she remained at Carlisle. Elizabeth almost at once dispatched Sir Francis Knollys and Lord Scrope to interview her. Scrope was governor of Carlisle and Warden of the West Marches, but had been absent when Mary arrived. Knollys was married to a niece of Elizabeth's mother, and had a privileged position in English court circles.

Some kind of investigation might help the English government to make up its mind, and the idea of an investigation, which occurred to Cecil at the outset, gradually came to prevail. A fortnight after her arrival in England Mary wrote to Elizabeth offering to purge herself of the calumnies of her enemies, and Elizabeth, in her reply, took this up, but indicated that she could not herself meet Mary: the latter must first be acquitted by agents of the English government, and not heard by Elizabeth in person. The other party chiefly concerned, namely

Moray and his faction, were all set to act as accusers of Mary, but Elizabeth at once reminded them that they also were accused, and must be ready to defend themselves against 'such weighty crimes and causes as the said Queen shall object against you'. Here was the prospect of a quasi-judicial investigation at which representatives of the English Queen would hear accusations and counter-accusations between the two parties.

Whatever terms and conditions might be laid down, Moray could hardly let his case go by default by refusing to appear and answer Mary's accusations, and he could answer her accusations only by counter-accusations. It was more difficult to persuade Mary to agree to an inquiry on Elizabeth's terms. She conceived the investigation as a preliminary to her restoration, and was not likely to co-operate unless it was going to have this character. In the belief that this was what was intended she was certainly encouraged by Elizabeth. When the latter first took up Mary's offer to justify herself, she undertook to prosecute Mary's adversaries according to the justice of Mary's cause, and Mary was told by Elizabeth's agent that she would be restored if her innocence were proved. Even in writing to Moray, Elizabeth said that nothing was to be done or intended to Mary's prejudice, and to Mary herself she said that she would hear the charges against her not as a judge but as Mary's friend, so that she could discover by what authority Mary's enemies had deprived her of her crown. 'I assure you', she wrote, 'I will do nothing to hurt you, but rather honour and aid you.' And, in a statement that she would 'agree her and her subjects and put her in her own country again according to God's calling,' she came very near to giving an unqualified promise of restoration.

It would be easy to see in this a design to lull Mary into an optimistic submission to an investigation which might in fact prove detrimental to her. Some contemporaries thought that there was such dishonesty. The Spanish ambassador said, 'They have signs and countersigns, and whilst they publicly write and do one thing, they secretly order another', and one Scot was reported to say that 'the Queen of England was using towards his mistress fair words and foul deeds.' But the apparent de-

ception, or at least equivocation, may really have arisen from a
difference of opinion between Elizabeth and her advisers. Elizabeth was genuinely more favourable to Mary than her councillors were, and while Cecil was sending assurances to Moray,
she was sending assurances to Mary. Elizabeth could hardly
defy humanity by sending another woman back to Scotland
to face execution as a criminal. Nor could she readily acquiesce
in even the deposition of Mary, for her own interest compelled
her to defend the rights of sovereigns, and she had not as yet
given formal recognition to Moray's government. Both instinct
and logic therefore inclined her to support Mary's case. If the
idea of detaining her without a fair trial had occurred to Elizabeth at an early stage it might not have been surprising, for
she herself, when heir presumptive to her sister, had had the
experience of confinement without trial. But, to do her justice,
it seems that she was only slowly and reluctantly driven to this
solution, though some of her ministers thought of it from the
outset. The divergence between Elizabeth and Cecil emerged
when Cecil wrote disapprovingly: 'The Queen's majesty . . .
meaneth to have the matter between the Queen of Scots and
her subjects . . . compounded with a certain manner of restitu-
tion of the Queen.'

On 13 July Mary had been moved from Carlisle to Bolton, in
Wensleydale; not, however, to bring her nearer to an interview
with Elizabeth, but to lessen the risk that she might escape. It
was on 28 July that she consented to the proposed inquiry. To
do so involved giving a command to her followers in Scotland
to enter on an armistice and to withdraw their application for
French help, and this directly strengthened Moray's position –
a very important point, in view of the readiness of the Marians to
continue the war. Besides, it was made clear that whichever
way the investigation went it would not result in Mary's unconditional restoration. It had been in Cecil's mind from the
beginning that the opportunity should be taken to drive a bargain advantageous to England. In his earliest observations on
the problem he had remarked that, should Mary be acquitted,
she should be required, 'in consideration of the benefit of acquit-

tal', to renounce her claim to the English throne. The fact that even her proven innocence was not to be followed by unconditional restoration shows how far away were any considerations of justice. Cecil's minutes are a completely cold-blooded assessment of the situation, with no suggestion whatever that there was any question of doing justice or even of being swayed by the evidence which might be produced. The notion of using Mary's necessity as England's opportunity to strike an advantageous bargain re-emerged when the plan for an investigation took shape. It was now laid down that, if Moray and his party should prove their charges, then either Mary should 'live in some convenient place without possessing her kingdom' or her restoration should at least be conditional on Moray's party being secured in their honours and estates. But if they could not prove their case, the restoration was still to be conditional : the conditions were that religion was to be the same in Scotland as in England, that there was to be a bond of amity between the two kingdoms, and that Mary would make no claims to Elizabeth's throne.

Elizabeth's ministers doubted whether it was practicable to provide sanctions to ensure that Mary would fulfil any such conditions, and Cecil said of them : 'How they shall be afterwards performed, wise men may doubt.' His misgivings about the possibility of binding Mary to any terms were justified, for no means were known to limit the sovereignty of a ruling monarch. At the same time, the prospect was not wholly illusory that a restored Mary might fulfil the first condition, namely uniformity in religion, by fostering the Book of Common Prayer in Scotland. The idea was not even a new one. There had been reports in 1562 that her uncle, the Cardinal of Lorraine, had urged her 'to embrace the religion of England'. And in 1567, not long after Darnley's murder, Maitland of Lethington had said that he did not despair of Mary's approving of Anglicanism : 'although she will not yield at the first, yet with progress of time that point shall be obtained.' Since then, Mary had been married to Bothwell by a Protestant bishop and she had taken the Scottish reformed Church under her protection. Now, on 8 August

1568, there came a report from Sir Francis Knollys, who was too puritanical to be easily deceived in such a matter:

Surely the Queen doth seem, outwardly, not only to favour this form, but also the chief articles, of the religion of the gospel, namely justification by faith only; and she heareth the faults of papistry revealed by preaching or otherwise, with contented ears and with gentle and weak replies.

This 'Anglican fit' on Mary's part was taken so seriously by Knollys that he was worried lest, in the event of her restoration, Scottish ministers should be subjected to the English vestiarian requirements which Puritans like himself detested, and it was taken so seriously by Mary herself that she felt obliged to make excuses: when some of her Roman Catholic friends complained about her behaviour, she reassured them, and a little later she wrote to King Philip:

If it is thought that I erred in participating in these prayers, at which I assisted because no other exercise of my religion was allowed me, I am ready to make such satisfaction as may be deemed necessary.

She put her opportunism squarely before Knollys:

Why, would you have me to lose France and Spain and all my friends in other places, by seeming to change my religion, and yet I am not assured that the Queen my good sister will be my assured friend?

This opportunism prevailed, and when Mary gave formal instructions to the commissioners who were to appear on her behalf there was an undertaking to consider conformity with England.

Even after the prospect of her immediate restoration had faded, she continued her flirtation with Anglicanism, for early in 1569 it was reported that she 'heard the English service with a book of the Psalms in English in her hand'. This was a very different Mary from the Mary who, on the scaffold in 1587, rejected the prayers of the Dean of Peterborough. Moray was characteristically censorious about what he regarded as insincerity:

Her resorting to the services of the Church of England serves her turn presently to move godly men to conceive a good opinion of her conformity. But I fear being restored to her government again . . . it should be one of the most difficult conditions to become good for that she should abandon the Mass.

But – leaving aside his air of superior rectitude – he was quite right in seeing the whole thing as a piece of opportunism.

The tripartite conference, at which English commissioners were to hear the cases put forward by Mary and Moray, finally opened on 4 October at York. It may be doubted whether anybody cared much whether Mary really *was* innocent or guilty, though to some it was a point of some importance whether she should be *proved* innocent or guilty. Essentially every party was concerned to exploit the situation for its own ends. Political considerations dominated, and if anyone had notions of justice in the abstract he said remarkably little about them. The question of punishing Mary as a criminal, should she be found guilty, was never really faced, and the possibility of simply liberating her unconditionally should she be proved innocent was, equally, never entertained.

The question was the purely political one – should she or should she not be restored to her throne? It may even be doubted if any of the parties really wanted the inquiry to be pushed to a decisive conclusion. Mary, indeed, hoped for a vindication and her restoration, but if she realized that was impossible, she preferred an equivocal outcome to unqualified condemnation as a criminal. Elizabeth, apart from her constitutional irresolution, had most to gain from an outcome which neither restored a rival nor necessitated a sentence on a sister queen. She would probably have preferred some kind of settlement which would save Mary from condemnation and even restore her to nominal sovereignty, but at the same time maintain Moray as effective ruler of Scotland. Moray, the third of the principals, had had previous experience of Elizabeth's unreliability, for in 1565 she had first secretly encouraged him to rebel against Mary and then had publicly repudiated and denounced him when his rebellion failed. He could not, therefore, risk accusing the woman who had been, and might again be, his lawful sovereign, unless he had some irrevocable guarantee for the security of his person, property, and authority if he should accuse Mary of murder and then find the charge not sustained.

The English delegation was headed by the Duke of Norfolk, the only duke in England and First Subject of the Realm. If Elizabeth was not going to be present herself, she could hardly have sent a more distinguished agent. Norfolk was accompanied by the Earl of Sussex and by Sir Ralph Sadler, a veteran of Anglo-Scottish negotiations who must have known Scotland as well as any man in England did. Moray went to York in person – the only one of the principals to appear, though he was nominally a commissioner for the infant King James. His four fellow commissioners included Bishop Adam Bothwell and the Earl of Morton, and with them were expert assessors – George Buchanan, the composer of the catalogue of Mary's crimes, Maitland of Lethington, the subtle Secretary of State, and two eminent lawyers. It was not without reason that Sadler, who knew the quality of the Scottish delegation, deplored the lack of legal skill on the English side. Mary had seven commissioners at York, the most notable of them John Lesley, Bishop of Ross, and Lord Herries: not one of the seven could be called a papist, for even Lesley seemed to Knollys to be 'almost a Protestant', and some of them had been conspicuous on the reforming side. On the other hand, none of Mary's representatives was a professional except Lesley, who was a canon lawyer.

If the principals were hesitant and perhaps uncertain of what they wanted out of the inquiry, it is also true that some of their agents had their own reasons for not wanting to push matters to extremes. Maitland wanted a reconciliation and Mary's restoration, partly because he looked above all to her recognition as heir to England – for which a condemned murderess could hardly hope – and partly perhaps because he feared disclosures of his own part in the plot against Darnley. It was remarked that he wished the matter to be settled 'in *dulce* manner'. As for Mary's representatives, at the beginning of the conference Lord Herries was willing to swear to say nothing but what was just and true, but not to swear to say all that he knew to be true : he was prepared, in short, to tell the truth but not the whole truth; and it was said of him that he 'labours for a reconciliation without odious accusations'. If this suggests that Mary's representatives possessed less than confidence in her innocence, it finds support in their readiness at a later stage in the proceedings to bring forward proposals for a compromise without having consulted her about them. And Lesley, another of her commissioners, was reported to say – admittedly three years later – that she had poisoned her first husband, consented to the murder of the second, married the murderer, and brought him to the field of Carberry to be murdered.

Elizabeth's commissioners were no less doubtful about the justice of their cause and hesitant about what they hoped to achieve. Sadler went to York an unhappy and perplexed man. 'Who is a tyrant?' he asked Cecil, 'Who may depose a tyrant?' Should the Scottish Queen be bound by the abdication which had been extorted from her? Norfolk, head of the English commission, was appalled by his task. 'This cause is the doubtfulest and dangerest that ever I dealt in; if you saw and heard the constant affirming of both sides, not without great stoutness, you would wonder.' He was sufficiently fair-minded to appreciate Moray's difficulty about proceeding to the accusation of murder, and also to see the inequity of refusing to let Mary be heard in person. But fair-mindedness was perhaps hardly a qualification for his task.

Besides, Norfolk soon had private ends of his own. It has been suggested that it was Maitland of Lethington who first implanted in his mind the idea that he might marry Mary, but, while Norfolk may not have been an over-intelligent man, it did not need much originality to think of this. The fact is that the possibility of Mary's re-marriage was being widely canvassed. And it was bound to be: a woman of twenty-six, Queen by right of one country, Queen Dowager of another, and heir to a third, with one infant son to inherit her rights, was bound to be a focus of matrimonial aspirations and calculations. Sir Francis Knollys was at this very time reflecting that, whatever Mary's future,

'All foreign practices would be avoided by an English marriage', and he specifically thought of George Carey, son of Lord Hunsdon, a cousin both of Elizabeth and of Knollys himself. Mary was as ready to grasp at this as at the Prayer Book. On 20 October Knollys reported that she would not 'greatly mislike' a marriage with a near kinsman of Elizabeth; and on the 21st she was indicating, for the first time, a readiness to be divorced from Bothwell.

However, if Norfolk was going to marry Mary, he wanted a queen regnant, not a prisoner or a pensioner, and he negotiated with Moray in the hope that the latter might accept a compromise, while he also encouraged Mary to aim at a triumphant acquittal. When Elizabeth later taxed Norfolk with his proposed marriage to Mary, he said he would rather go to the Tower than marry a woman with whom 'he could not be sure of his pillow'. He had perhaps been listening to Lesley telling how she had disposed of two husbands and had tried to dispose of a third. But his marriage plan was serious enough, even although he had seen the Casket Letters, one of which he characterized as 'a horrible and long letter, of her own hand as they said, containing foul matter and abominable to be either thought of or to be written by a prince'. But it should be remembered that Knollys was equally convinced of Mary's guilt and yet, godly man as he was, he did not see guilt in a queen as an obstacle to respectable matrimony. This is another illustration of the fact that men did not much care whether Mary was guilty or innocent.

Both the accusations of Mary and her defence fall broadly into two phases, corresponding almost exactly to the work done at York and that done at Westminster. At York, when Moray had not yet received any guarantee for his own security, he was concerned, publicly at least, only to justify his own rebellion, and this he attempted to do by laying his emphasis on the marriage to Bothwell when he was under suspicion as Darnley's murderer and on Mary's failure to prosecute Bothwell for that crime. Mary's defence at this stage was that before she married Bothwell he had been formally acquitted of the Darnley murder, that the marriage had been commended to her by a large body of lords, that she had surrendered at Carberry on the promise that she would have the renewed obedience of her subjects if she abandoned Bothwell, and that the abdication had been made under threat of death. It was added – and it was a good point – that not a tenth of the nobility of Scotland had taken part in James's coronation. This was all substantially true, and was an able defence. Sussex remarked that 'her proofs will fall out best, as is thought.' All in all, the discussions at York seem to have been free from acrimony, for there were 'merry and pleasant speeches' among men who for the most part were old acquaintances. While the real obstacle to a conclusive discussion and a serious conflict was the inability of the English commissioners to give Moray the guarantee he wanted, the whole tone seems to have been amicable.

Perhaps Elizabeth thought it was too inconclusive and too amicable. The Norfolk marriage project led to a hardening of her attitude towards Mary, but the main reason why she gave instructions on 3 November that proceedings should be trans- ferred to Westminster may have been Mary's comparative success at York. The move to Westminster meant that Mary was further from the scene, while Moray had direct access to Elizabeth and her ministers. There was much more formality in the new situation. The English now produced a far more impressive tribunal, containing two marquises, about a third of England's earls, and officials like Cecil. When proceedings began at Westminster on 25 November the atmosphere was no longer one of friendly and informal talks, and Mary's com- missioners, in particular, further from their mistress and greatly outnumbered, must have felt their task much more difficult.

Moray now received the assurance he sought – that, should he prove Mary's guilt, his position would be secured and Mary would not be restored. Thus fortified, he proceeded, in his 'Eik' or addition to his earlier charges, to accuse Mary of being a party to the murder of Darnley. Mary's defence now was that the whole rebellion against her had been based on false accu- sations, that the catalogue of her crimes was a mere pretext to justify it, and that the real cause was that 'they [the rebels] were aware that she could use the privilege of the laws, always granted to the kings of that realm before, and make revocation before her full age of twenty-five years, and this was a way to take from them the livings before given them'. The rebellion, it will be recalled, had occurred after Mary had entered her twenty-fifth year, the year in which a Scottish sovereign was accustomed to make a revocation of crown grants. The suspicion that the prospect of a revocation may have lain behind Mary's troubles in 1567 is confirmed by some remarks of Sir James Melville in his *Memoirs*, as well as by the seriousness with which this matter was argued in the proceedings at Westminster.

No one who reviews the events of the inquiry can assert that Mary received fair or equitable treatment, at any rate after the early stages at York. The principal injustice was the refusal to allow her to appear in person. At the outset, Mary asked for an interview with Elizabeth herself, and returned to this request again and again. She pointed out that when Moray had been a refugee, after the Chaseabout Raid in 1565, he had been received by Elizabeth. Elizabeth's unvarying reply was that it was inconsistent with her honour to receive Mary as long as she was under suspicion, but it is not easy to follow her reasoning. There can be no doubt about the truth: apart from Elizabeth's own shrinking from a personal interview, her ministers were determined that Mary should not be allowed the opportunity to bring her charm into play. Cecil had read the reports by Knollys of the impression which had been made on him by the 'eloquent tongue, ready wit, and constant courage' of this 'notable woman', and it must have been brought home to him that Mary must on no account be permitted to appear in person and influence English commissioners. An agent who reported to Cecil a little later, in February 1569, said explicitly, 'I must advise that very few should have access to or conference with this lady' for she had 'an alluring grace, a pretty Scottish accent, and a searching wit'. The inequity in the treatment of Mary became even more marked when proceedings moved from York to Westminster, for as soon as Moray arrived in London he was received by Elizabeth, but she continued to refuse to see the Scottish Queen.

Apart from this, in the proceedings themselves there were episodes which look like underhand dealing. The first of them had taken place only six days after the opening of the conference at York. Moray was still refusing to bring forward a formal accusation of Mary until he had a guarantee that, should he prove his case, she would not be restored. But, while he was still awaiting such a guarantee, a curious step was taken. An approach was made, not by the members of his commission, but by his four professional assessors, to Norfolk, Sussex, and Sadler, whom the Scots said they wanted to meet not as commissioners but, as Norfolk described it, in private and secret conference. And it was in these quite irregular circumstances that the Casket Letters were first shown to Elizabeth's representatives, by Scots whose action could subsequently have been repudiated by Moray had he thought fit.

The obvious reluctance of Moray to submit his evidence to serious challenge came out even more forcibly in the latter stages of the proceedings. After a few days at Westminster, Mary's representatives, Lesley and Herries, declared that if Elizabeth persisted in her refusal to allow Mary to appear in person the conference must be considered to be at an end, and they in effect walked out. It was thereafter, and only thereafter, that the full-scale indictment of Mary, the Book of Articles, was produced, and with it the Casket Letters. The latter thus made an appearance officially only when there was no one present to challenge their authenticity. The failure to submit Moray's evidence to real challenge was, of course, one consequence of the peculiar character of the investigations. Because the proceedings were not judicial, not those of a court of law, the evidence was never subjected to cross-examination as it would have been in normal legal process. Equally, no witnesses were called on either side. It is, of course, doubtful if there could have been a legal tribunal with appropriate competence. Not only did Mary contend from first to last that as a sovereign princess she could not be legally tried by any tribunal, but even as a suspected criminal she did not come under the jurisdiction of a tribunal in a foreign land. It was, indeed, only step by step that the investigation had taken on the character of an inquiry into Mary's guilt.

In the final stage, at Hampton Court on 14 December, Elizabeth assembled a large number of notables to hear her justification of her refusal to receive Mary in person. The responsibility for the breakdown of the conference was then thrown on Mary's commissioners, and the implication was that they had been unable to put up a defence. There was indeed a deadlock, but it was not as it was represented: Elizabeth refused to let Mary see the Book of Articles until she had promised to answer it, and Mary refused to promise to answer it until she had seen it. There were still discussions about a possible compromise between Mary and Moray, but this is no proof that Englishmen who had seen Moray's evidence and accepted Elizabeth's arguments still believed that Mary could put up a good defence if the proceedings were reopened. On the contrary, the opinion of Englishmen who had seen Moray's evidence – his unchallenged evidence – was hardening against Mary. Her representatives learned on 28 December from Norfolk, Leicester, and Cecil that their judgments were almost confirmed in favour of Mary's adversaries. This meant that, if Mary was not going to resign her crown voluntarily, her detention in England was almost the only possible course. The idea of detaining her had been in the minds of Elizabeth's advisers from an early stage, and Sussex had written from York on 22 October, 'I think surely no end can be made good for England except the person of the Scots Queen be detained, by one means or another, in England.' Exactly two months later, Cecil, in one of his memoranda, envisaged such a detention. He pointed out that even if Moray's party had been accessories to the murder of Darnley and the Bothwell marriage, that did not extinguish Mary's own guilt.

Even so, there was no sentence, and the decision for Mary's continued detention was arrived at tacitly. It was on 10 January that Elizabeth announced her inconclusive finding. Nothing had been proved against Moray to impair his honour, nothing had been proved against Mary to cause Elizabeth to conceive any evil opinion of her. Both were innocent. But the two were differently treated. Moray was at once given liberty to depart for Scotland, with a loan of £5,000 in his pocket. Yet, when Mary's commissioners said that if he had licence to go she also should have licence to go, no such licence was given. That she should be allowed to depart seems never to have been seriously considered. This treatment of Moray and Mary was the solution which Cecil had suggested as early as 21 November: 'the Queen of Scots to remain deprived of her crown and the State [of Scotland] continue as it is.' It was a double success for England: Mary was detained, and to that extent rendered less dangerous; but she was not condemned and to that extent was not driven, in despair of justice in England, to seek help elsewhere. A final attempt to persuade her to demit the crown and agree voluntarily to live in England had been made without success. She requested 'the person who wrote her to resign to trouble her no more with such a request, for she is resolved to die rather than do it, and the last word in her life shall be that of a Queen of Scotland'.

7 Captivity

The inconclusive 'sentence' of 10 January 1569 seems definitive in the light of our hindsight, but it did not seem so at the time. The door to Mary's restoration to her throne had by no means been finally closed. For one thing, the English decision to detain her meant an end of the armistice which had begun when the inquiry at York opened, and was followed by the resumption of civil war in Scotland. Mary's case, which had impressed those in England who had heard it equitably presented, was cogent enough to make an influential party in Scotland fight for it for three more years. Whether a victory for Mary's Scottish supporters would have caused the English government to release her is another matter, but for one reason or another talk of her restoration was revived from time to time during almost the whole period of her captivity, and there were two phases in which such talk was not unrealistic – in 1569–70 and again between 1581 and 1584.

Six months after the Hampton Court decision the Queen's party in Scotland were putting forward for consideration by parliament a proposal that she should be divorced from Bothwell as a preliminary to her marriage to Norfolk and her restoration. In that same summer of 1569 Elizabeth was trying out various restoration proposals: if Mary would not ratify her abdication and live in retirement in England, she might rule jointly with James or might be restored as sole titular ruler, with guarantees in the matters of religion and security for Moray and his party. It was still true, moreover, that Mary had not made any resignation of her claim to the English throne, and there had not even been a declaration by any English authority against her rights as Elizabeth's heir. Finally, she remained all the time as attractive as ever as a bride for ambitious suitors, whether on the Continent or in England. Even before the proceedings at Westminster were over it was evident that Norfolk was not without competitors and that intrigues for a continental marriage would resume: on 3 January 1569 Bishop Lesley, writing to the Earl of Arundel, mentioned that the King of Spain had empowered his ambassador to offer three possible Hapsburg bridegrooms – Philip himself (who had been widowed again with the death of Elizabeth of France in 1568), his cousin the Archduke Charles, and his half-brother Don John of Austria.

However, whether Mary was to remain in England temporarily or permanently, arrangements had to be made for the conditions in which she would live. On 20 January Elizabeth reminded her that her affairs were 'not so clear as they should be'. This implied a threat against an accused but unacquitted prisoner, and it was the background for the remarks which followed it in Elizabeth's letter: understanding, so she said, that Mary disliked Bolton Castle, she had prepared another place for her and had ordered her to be escorted there. Word of a likely removal had evidently come to Mary's ears before that letter was written, for on 21 January Henry Knollys (deputizing for Francis, who had just lost his wife) informed Cecil that Mary had said she would not remove 'without violence' and added malevolently 'but we shall know the certainty this night'. Next day Mary wrote to Elizabeth, reproaching her for refusing to see her and for detaining her. It was on the 26th that Mary was actually taken from Bolton, 'with an evil will and much ado', and reached Ripon. While subjected to this forcible removal, she was meantime being pressed to repudiate allegations, circulated by her party in Scotland, that England was going to establish control over Scotland, and she 'refuseth them plainly for none of hers'. Knollys reported next day, 'we forbore troubling her thereon last night for her weariness after the journey and late arrival at her lodging'. On the 28th, Francis Knollys added that Mary admitted that she had authorized a proclamation to stir up the Scots against Moray and had approved an allegation that Moray had promised to deliver her son to the English, but she denied that she had been responsible for propaganda which slandered Elizabeth.

The destination in January 1569 was Tutbury Castle in Staffordshire, a vast medieval pile which had fallen into disrepair. Situated on a hill, it was exposed and draughty, but it was also damp from surrounding marshy ground. Mary loathed the unhealthy place. However, it was only one of many residences in which she was lodged at one time or another. From 1569 to 1585 she was mostly at Sheffield Castle, with intermissions at Wingfield Manor and Chatsworth when the sanitary conditions of the time dictated the cleansing of Sheffield and with a visit now and again to the baths at Buxton for the sake of her health. Fresh air and outdoor exercise were not entirely ruled out, but the partial deprivation of them was the most serious loss suffered by a woman who had taken so much pleasure in open-air recreation, and it had a serious effect on her physical wellbeing. But there was also a profound psychological effect from exchanging the life of courts and public appearances to which she had been accustomed for a prison and the company of a very restricted circle of people.

Mary's keeper, down to 1585, was George Talbot, Earl of Shrewsbury, a very wealthy noble fourteen years older than Mary. His instructions were that she was to be treated as a queen, with reverence fitting her degree and her nearness in blood to Elizabeth, but on the other hand he was to beware lest she try to gain influence over him or attempt her escape, and no one was to be in her company save her retinue and others who received special permission. Mary was treated with formal respect, sitting under a royal cloth of state, and she had her own household of thirty or forty persons. She appointed them herself, and she must have drawn some comfort from the fact – highly creditable to her – that she never had any difficulty in keeping her retainers; she was always a kind mistress, and her servants seldom wanted to leave her. Shrewsbury, extremely loyal to his own queen, was fussy about the security of his charge, but he seems from time to time to have stretched a point

in her favour. Any gaoler of Mary had, of course, a good motive
for avoiding undue harshness: at any time Elizabeth might die
and she would be Queen of England, though this consideration
became less cogent after James grew to manhood and Mary's
health and expectation of life diminished. Shrewsbury's wife,
Bess of Hardwick, eight years older than he, was a dominating
character, shrewd and calculating in business and something
of a termagant in the household. While Mary and she had a
good deal of each other's company, the countess's somewhat
masculine character was not suited for coming to terms with a
woman so essentially feminine as Mary.

Mary's person and her surroundings were far too closely
guarded to admit any possibility of escape without external
assistance in force. All her correspondence, too, was supposed
to pass through Shrewsbury's hands. However, as the expenses
of her establishment were borne by the English government,
she was able to use income from her revenues as Queen Dowager
of France to maintain secret contact with English Roman Catholics and with plotters on the Continent, and she was fertile in
ideas for conveying letters surreptitiously. She became an in-
veterate plotter, and as the years went by and her declining
health made her less fit for active exercise, intrigue became something of a hobby and pastime, alongside the embroidery on
which she spent many hours, sometimes in company with Lady
Shrewsbury. Yet only too often her agents were beaten by the
intelligence service of Elizabeth's government and her supposed
secrets discovered. Her brother-in-law, Charles IX of France,
remarked in 1572 with some prescience: 'Ah, the poor fool
will never cease until she lose her head. In faith, they will put
her to death. I see it is her own fault and folly, I see no remedy
for it.'

It is hard to acquit her of folly when one reflects that her
situation from 1569 onwards was not necessarily less happy
than life in Scotland would have been. Had she gone back to
Scotland as Queen, whether under formal limitations or not,
she would inevitably have had to depend on some faction and
would therefore have been subject to limitations in the exercise

of her regal power. It was remarked several times, and Mary herself must have realized it, that there was no party in Scotland which would put her interests before its own. Cecil may have been exaggerating when he said, more than once, that if she went back neither she nor the prince would 'have long continuance', but the danger was there, as had been abundantly shown in the past. The Englishmen who met the Scots at York took as poor a view of them as Cecil did. Sussex had said in his letter of 22 October that the two factions 'for their private causes, toss between them the crown and public affairs of Scotland . . . and care neither for the mother nor the child (as I think before God) but to serve their own ends'. And Norfolk said that many of the Scots sought wholly to serve their own private ends, caring not 'what becomes of either King or Queen'. Cecil returned to his argument later: Mary, he said, should be brought to see that if she were restored, the Hamiltons and their dependants, like Huntly and Argyll, would be in control, and neither she nor her son, he repeated, would 'have long continuance', whereas she would be safe in England.

It is true that Cecil – unlike his mistress – seems to have had a particular spite at the Hamiltons, and that Englishmen may have been too ready to sneer at the politics of their neighbours, but a Scot whose attitude was fair and detached could say much the same: 'some drew to both the factions that desired never to see either King or Queen in an established estate.' Perhaps Mary was better out of it all. Would it really have been in her interest to face the possibility of a repetition of the Riccio, the Darnley, or the Bothwell episodes? It would have been quite reasonable to calculate that she might do better to remain in England and exploit her claims to build up a party which might in the end win two kingdoms for her. It is not difficult, of course, to see Mary's difficulty in formally and voluntarily accepting her deposition. As she had declared in 1569, she was resolved rather to die than to resign her rights. She had remarked earlier that if Elizabeth was a lion, she was of the same breed.

It has to be remembered, too, in assessing the advantages in Mary's position after 1568, that she was not yet defamed in England. Although the accusations against her had been made known to a good number of Englishmen at Westminster and Hampton Court, they had not been published, and none of the proceedings had been public. No doubt reports circulated, and there was even a certain amount of material in print. Robert Sempill's *Ane Declaration of the Lordis Just Querrell*, published in Scotland in 1567, gave the case against Mary, partly on constitutional arguments but partly on her immorality, and John Pikeryng's *Horestes*, a play presented at the English court late in 1567, had been transparently an account of Mary's doings under the guise of Clytemnestra. But when Shrewsbury received his instructions for her detention he was told to warn her that, if she made trouble or if she uttered any speeches about Elizabeth's actions towards her which reflected on Elizabeth's honour, it might cause the English Queen to publish 'her whole causes and doings to the world'. This was a threat, but it was also a promise, and might have been an incentive to good behaviour. Elizabeth, it must be said, kept her word. As long as Mary acted with discretion Elizabeth declined to authorize the publication of the case against her. Not only so, but when 'French' Paris, the one-time servitor of Bothwell, was arrested in Scotland in August 1569, Elizabeth pleaded for the deferment of his execution so that he could be thoroughly examined, in the hope that the truth would emerge; but the government of Moray caused him to be executed before Elizabeth's plea arrived. It would seem that the English Queen was not wholly acting a part when she withheld judgment on Mary and refused to have her formally condemned. As we shall see, it was only after the revelations of Mary's implication in the Ridolfi plot of 1571 that the evidence against her was released.

Mary's prospects, and the schemes which in one way or another concerned her, were all along closely linked with the international situation and affected by its changes. Right at the outset, indeed while the inquiry was still going on, events had taken a turn which, it seemed, might work to her advantage. At the end of 1568, when ships carrying money destined for the Spanish forces in the Netherlands had put into English ports to

escape pirates, Elizabeth had seized the money. Alva, the governor of the Netherlands, retaliated by seizing English ships and
goods. It looked as if there must be war between England and
Spain, which would surely, so Mary thought, mean the landing
in England of a Spanish force on which she counted to overthrow
Elizabeth and set her up as Queen. Nothing came of this, and
indeed no serious Spanish attempt was ever to be made at the
invasion of England until after Mary was dead, but the possibility was never long absent from her mind.

It was also true that, as Cecil had foreseen, Mary almost at
once became the focus of plots within England itself, though
these plots were nearly always linked with proposals for col-
laboration with France or Spain and the Papacy. The fact is that,
if the decision of 1569 could in some ways be interpreted as
being to Mary's advantage, it is hard to see that it brought much
gain to Elizabeth. Undoubtedly it prevented Mary from becom-
ing in person the figurehead of a crusade by a foreign power
against England, and, by being able at any time to threaten to
release Mary, Elizabeth acquired some influence over the Scottish government; but these were meagre advantages to set off
against the constant stimulus given to English plotters and the
constant anxiety caused to Elizabeth by the presence of a rival
queen within her realm.

In the first phase, in 1569, Mary's cause was supported by a
very mixed band of conspirators, some of whom wanted the
restoration of Roman Catholicism, some of whom aimed merely
at overthrowing Cecil and some perhaps simply at ending the
perils of a disputed succession by securing the recognition of
Mary as heir to the crown. Mary had so many well-wishers in
England at this point – many of them admittedly for purely
selfish reasons – that one feels the force of Elizabeth's refusal
to publish the evidence against her, as well as the results of the
activity of her defenders, notably John Lesley, whose *Defence* of
Mary was printed in 1569. One of the roots of the plotting in
England was the projected marriage to Norfolk, which had
never been lost sight of after it was first mooted at York in
October 1568. In the marriage itself there would have been

nothing either unreasonable or traitorous towards Elizabeth, especially as Norfolk was not a Roman Catholic and indeed had a strain of puritanism in his upbringing, but in the eyes of those who pressed it it was clearly intended to involve Mary's restoration to Scotland and her recognition as Elizabeth's heir, and the conservative peers who associated with Norfolk saw it as a means of wresting power from Cecil and the ultra-Protestant and anti-Spanish faction.

Beyond this, however, lay the activities of the northern earls, Northumberland and Westmorland, who carried their conservatism to the extent of planning the restoration of Roman Catholicism, if necessary with foreign help; and their schemes were incompatible with the continuance of Elizabeth's rule or even of her life. Mary was in touch with this group as well as with the more moderate men, including for a time Leicester, who aimed primarily at ending the ascendancy of Cecil. Elizabeth weaned Leicester from the conspiracy and tried to detach Norfolk, but the duke failed to respond and found himself in danger of being drawn to lend countenance to armed revolt. This he refused to face, so he obeyed a command to come to court and was sent to the Tower on 11 October 1569.

Norfolk, Mary, and the Spanish ambassador all advised the northern earls against action, but when Elizabeth summoned them to court the result was the outbreak of a rebellion, in November. The rebels made for Tutbury to release Mary, but she was hurried off to Coventry before they arrived, and they were afraid to venture beyond Yorkshire. The Midlands and the south of the country provided ample levies of loyal forces to counter theirs, and, faced with the certainty of defeat, they broke up without a serious battle. The leaders crossed the Border into Scotland, but over 500 of their humble followers were put to death.

The Earl of Northumberland was held a prisoner by Moray, who tried to bargain his surrender in return for financial assistance and full recognition of the Scottish régime. Before Elizabeth could come to terms Moray was murdered (23 January 1570). The situation led to English intervention in Scotland, of a somewhat peculiar and limited nature. The Earl of Sussex and Sir William Drury conducted military operations to punish Borderers who had harboured fugitives from the late northern rebellion and to despoil the lands of some of Mary's supporters. Elizabeth also used her influence with the Scottish leaders to have the Earl of Lennox, Darnley's father, appointed as Regent (July). But Elizabeth had intervened in these ways with a view less to extinguishing Mary's hopes in Scotland than to creating conditions in which she could be restored under strict limitations. In the negotiations that followed we see the significance of the composition of the Marian party in Scotland, which was now appealing to Elizabeth for Mary's restoration. For one thing, it still contained at least half of the notables: the signatories of a letter to Elizabeth in March 1570 included ten earls and fourteen lords. More than that, it included some old friends to England and to the Reformation, among them now Maitland of Lethington, who had as good a right as anyone in King James's party had to appeal for the continuance of the Anglo-Scottish *entente*, and in his mind Mary's restoration was to be considered in that context. Elizabeth favoured Mary's restoration at this point partly with a view to neutralizing France and preventing that power from intervening in Scotland on Mary's behalf. Cecil was sent to negotiate with Mary, and representatives of the King's party were summoned from Scotland. The latter came, early in 1571, but were far from enthusiastic, for they felt their own position incompatible with Mary's restoration on any terms. They made the excuse that they must first consult a parliament, which was due to meet in May. Before anything further could be done, events happened which altered Elizabeth's attitude to Mary and put her restoration out of the question for a long time.

Elizabeth's relations with Roman Catholics, both at home and abroad, had entered a new phase with the papal bull excommunicating her, issued in February 1570 and brought into England in May. On top of this came the Ridolfi plot. Ridolfi, a Florentine banker who had carried on business in London, had acted as a papal agent and had dealt with the Spanish ambassador and with Lesley on behalf of Mary. He was one of the many over-credulous or over-optimistic Roman Catholic agents who could sketch hare-brained schemes and assume that foreign powers and English and Scottish magnates would be so reckless as to commit themselves without reservations and without guarantees. Again and again some quite insignificant agent could conjure up the prospect that a foreign army of 10,000, or even 20,000, men was ready to land in England, Scotland, or Ireland. Some of these agents were far more dangerous to their friends than to their enemies.

At this stage, Norfolk, released from the Tower but under surveillance and sworn not to deal further for a marriage with Mary, had in fact remained in touch with her and also with Lesley, though probably not traitorously and quite possibly with a view to exercising a restraining influence. Yet he was to some extent drawn into the plot, though not as far as Ridolfi and Lesley represented. Ridolfi's plan was for the landing of a Spanish army sent by Alva from the Netherlands and a simultaneous rising by Norfolk and the English Roman Catholics. Ridolfi went to the Continent in March 1571 to complete the arrangements, armed mainly with grossly overoptimistic assessments of the situation in England and of the attitudes of Mary and Norfolk. He found that Alva was cautious and was disposed to insist that the English rising must precede the invasion. Letters were intercepted, the whole thing was discovered, and Cecil made the most of it, in the first place to discredit Norfolk. The duke was arrested and tried for treason, on the grounds of his attempts to marry a rival claimant to Elizabeth's throne, the assistance he had given to refugees from the northern rebellion, the fact that he had remitted some money to Mary's supporters in Scotland, and his part in a conspiracy for the deposition of Elizabeth with foreign help. Tried with the customary injustice of English treason trials of the period, Norfolk was convicted. He admitted that he had received a letter from the Pope, but insisted that he had never written to the Pope and that if a letter had gone in his name it must have been a forgery. After prolonged hesitation on the part of the Queen, he was executed

(2 June 1572). John Lesley, who had long been regarded with suspicion by the English government, had also been arrested, and had made admissions which went a long way to incriminate his mistress.

It has become something of a fashion to contend that all the Roman Catholic conspiracies in England, from Ridolfi's to the Gunpowder Plot, were fabrications by the English government, designed to discredit the Roman cause or sometimes merely to bring about the downfall of some individual. Mary's experience had already shown, and was again to show, that fabrication and trickery could be resorted to, and there is, besides, clear evidence that some adventurers were so lacking in loyalty to either Mary or Elizabeth that they could be brought either by bribes or threats to play double parts. It is also true that the animosities between different factions of the Roman Catholics were such that accusations of double-dealing were somewhat freely made. The inexplicable thing is that the plotters placed any confidence at all in men who were not wholly above suspicion. However, reviewing the history of half a century, not only in Britain but on the Continent, there is such ample evidence of papal encouragement for revolution and assassination that neither Mary nor the English Roman Catholics seem cast for the parts of injured innocents. In this case, quite apart from what Lesley, Mary's agent, disclosed – admittedly under conditions of strict imprisonment in the Tower – papers found when Dumbarton Castle had been captured from Mary's supporters in April 1571 provide evidence of her dealings with Alva.

After this episode, Elizabeth not only abandoned the current negotiations for Mary's restoration, but withdrew her opposition to the defamation of Mary and permitted the publication of incriminating matter. Before 1 November 1571 the Latin text of Buchanan's *Detectio Mariae Reginae* was printed in London, with, appended to it, a Latin *Actio contra Mariam* and three of the Casket Letters. The *Actio* had been written by Thomas Wilson, later Secretary of State. Wilson next translated the *Detectio* and the *Actio* into what he called 'Scottish', and added all eight Casket Letters. This publication, as *Ane Detectioun*, appeared in two editions, within a month of the Latin original. Meanwhile a genuinely Scottish edition of the *Detectio* had been printed at St Andrews, and there were editions in Germany and France. It was only with the issue of this hostile publicity that Mary, for the first time, stood before the world publicly indicted as a murderess. No such public indictment had emerged at the time of her first trial.

If Elizabeth was prepared to authorize these publications, her subjects were ready to draw their inferences. Already, in a parliament before the Ridolfi revelations, there had been a bill which in effect took away from Mary and her heirs any title to succeed to England. Now, in May 1572, when parliament met again, members clamoured for the execution of Mary, as well as for that of Norfolk. Mary, it was declared, had 'heaped up together all the sins of the licentious sons of David, adulteries, murders, conspiracies, treasons, and blasphemies against God'; she had instigated the rebellion in the north and had practised with Ridolfi for the invasion of England. The influence of the *Detectio* is to be seen in the exclamation of one member that she was the most notorious whore in all the world. But if Elizabeth was so reluctant to take the final, irrevocable step with her own subject, Norfolk, she was not likely to approve of the execution of a sister queen. Not only so, but the Royal Assent was withheld from a bill which passed both Houses, declaring it treason to support Mary's title to the English crown, providing for her trial by the peers of England if she plotted against Elizabeth again, and authorizing her death without trial if any insurrection took place in her favour.

These revelations of Mary's guilt also had a bearing on the English attitude to the two parties in Scotland. Because of Mary's plotting for the overthrow and death of Elizabeth, the latter could not now agree to restore her to authority, or even to liberty; Elizabeth, in making this point, declared that if the Marians would give up resistance she would plead for the security of their lives and property, but if they refused to do so she would aid the King's party. This was in October 1571. Should Elizabeth thus come down decisively on the side of the King's party, one possible way of dealing with Mary would be to send her back to Scotland to receive justice there. An essential preliminary to any such move was to come to terms with France. That country might have been expected to act in Mary's favour, but a by-product of the Ridolfi Plot, exploited to the full by Cecil, was the revelation that Mary was depending on Spain and not on France. This facilitated the framing of the Treaty of Blois, concluded between England and France in April 1572 and making no reference to Mary.

In the following August the massacre of St Bartholomew's Eve raised the hopes of Mary's supporters, who saw the possibilities if France adopted a militant anti-Protestant policy abroad as well as at home; but its more important effect was to embitter English feeling against Mary and at the same time to encourage Elizabeth's resolution to bring about a settlement in Scotland before France might intervene there. In September and October Elizabeth contemplated handing Mary over to the Scottish government, but after the death on 28 October of the Regent, Mar (who had succeeded Lennox in September 1571), English policy was directed instead to bringing about a settlement in Scotland without reference to Mary at all. The fact was that Elizabeth was less moved emotionally by the massacre than her subjects were, and she saw no reason in the long run to alter her policy of keeping Mary in detention in England. In 1573 English artillery was sent to Scotland to reduce Edinburgh Castle, the last stronghold of Mary's supporters, and the war between the King's party and the Queen's party came to an end. The Earl of Morton was now Regent, and as long as his rule lasted there were no prospects for Mary in Scotland.

On the international front, too, there was a period which was less eventful and less encouraging for Mary, because there was a kind of equilibrium. English Roman Catholic refugees on the Continent agitated for action against Elizabeth, and the Pope, too, was eager that Roman Catholic sovereigns, especially Philip of Spain, should take up 'the Enterprise of England' as a crusade.

But Philip feared that war with England, even though in favour of a French Queen Dowager, might involve him in war with France as well, and he knew that action by him against Elizabeth would stimulate her assistance to his rebellious subjects in the Netherlands. Elizabeth's own diplomatic skill, combined with Philip's caution and the reluctance of his governors in the Netherlands to allow troops to be withdrawn for an attack on England, maintained an uneasy peace.

The most promising situation for Mary at any time between 1573 and 1580 developed after 1576, when Don John of Austria, Philip's half-brother, became governor of the Netherlands. Something of a European hero after his victory over the Turks at Lepanto in 1571, but still under thirty years of age, he seemed the ideal leader for another crusade, this time against heretical England. The general idea was that after making peace in the Netherlands he would invade England, free Mary, and rule the country as her consort. But Don John's success in the Netherlands was never so complete as to make the Enterprise of England opportune, and Philip, cautious as ever, did not long give full support to the project. Yet for a year or two fears and hopes centred on Don John, and when he died in October 1579 Elizabeth's ministers thought the event a salutary miracle.

The final phase of the intrigues involving Mary may be said to begin in 1580, for from that point until her death plot succeeded plot, and conspiracy was almost incessant until the climax which led to her second trial and her execution. In a general way, the situation was shaped by a heightening of the militancy of papal policy. For some years Roman Catholic missionaries had been reaching England from the seminary at Douai, and in 1580 they were reinforced by the more dedicated and aggressive Jesuits. This activity led to a fresh wave of alarm and anger in England, and not without reason, for the missionaries rallied the English Romanists and put an end to the possibility that they would be quietly and gradually absorbed into the Church of England. To make matters worse, a papal pronouncement was issued in 1580 that anyone assassinating Elizabeth 'with the pious intention of doing God service, not

only does not sin, but gains merit'. The practical outcome of
such a policy was illustrated in two attempts, the second of them
successful, to murder William of Orange, the leader of the Protestants in the Netherlands.

In 1580, events in Scotland too had taken a turn which offered
possibilities both of a base being found there for the enterprise
of England and also of the restoration of Mary to the Scottish
throne by negotiation. The regency of Morton, who had excluded former Marians from office, came to an end in 1578,
and men began to wonder what influences were going to shape
the policy of King James (now twelve) as he emerged from
tutelage. Morton did not finally lose control of affairs until the
end of 1580, but already there had been established in Scotland
a faction, or at least an interest, which was disposed to challenge
every aspect of Morton's policy – his antagonism to Mary, his
resolute adherence to Protestantism, and his constancy to an
English alliance. The opposition to Morton found a leader in
Esmé Stewart, a first cousin of Darnley, who arrived from France
in September 1579 and rapidly won the devotion of the adoles-
cent King, by whom he was created Earl of Lennox and subsequently Duke. Esmé's real objectives were most likely personal
and dynastic – he was, after a childless great-uncle, the King's
nearest kinsman – and there is no reason to believe that his
arrival in Scotland was designed as a move in a Roman Catholic
enterprise. But there were those who thought they could use
him in the papal interest.

Mary herself took some initiative by proposing in 1581,
through the Duke of Guise, a 'scheme of association' whereby
she should be restored as joint sovereign with her son. The proposal, which was to be brought up in various forms over the
next two or three years, seemed superficially to have much to
commend it. To James it offered a degree of formal recognition
which could never be forthcoming otherwise as long as his
mother lived. To Elizabeth it offered the prospect of settling
the problem of Mary and, provided that the terms were sufficiently firm and faithfully carried out, rendering her innocuous.
To Mary, who was not likely to believe that her sovereignty

could be restricted, it was merely a step towards the recovery of real power. James might have accepted the scheme provided that Mary remained in England, and Mary at one stage professed to be ready to do so – but only so that she would be available to join a Roman Catholic army of invasion when one came. It is doubtful, in fact, if the interests of the various parties could have been reconciled.

But those who thought they could use Lennox in the Roman Catholic cause included the usual band of credulous and optimistic priests, this time the English Jesuit Parsons and two Scottish Jesuits, Crichton and Hay, who worked closely with the Spanish ambassador in London, Mendoza. Glowing reports appeared that not only Lennox but some of the leading Scottish earls would accept Spanish help to bring about James's conversion or, if he refused, to depose him. Early in 1582 an ambitious, but quite unrealistic, scheme was hatched: a large force was to be sent from the Continent, Lennox would put himself at its head and, after securing Scotland, would raise the Roman Catholics in England. As Mendoza put it in a letter to Philip, Mary was 'virtually the mainspring of the war, without whose opinion and countenance Lennox and others will do nothing'. James himself showed an opportunism worthy of his mother in her more diplomatic days: he wrote to her in polite terms, he also wrote to Guise, and he gave secret interviews to some of the clerical emissaries. His position was far too insecure to enable him to take a strong line, and he calculated that his equivocal attitude might assure his future should Spain take the Enterprise up seriously and carry it through with success.

Lennox, whether justly or not, was denounced in Scotland as an agent of the Counter-Reformation, and in a *coup d'état* known as the Ruthven Raid (August 1582) was displaced by an ultra-Protestant faction who controlled the King for ten months. He withdrew to France and died there the next year. Elizabeth had remained more or less neutral in relation to Lennox: after all, he represented French influence, and at this stage England was so closely allied with France that the Queen was renewing her dalliance with the French King's younger brother. She had

probably been right not to take action against one whose ecclesiastical standpoint was at worst equivocal and who was associated with her ally, France, rather than with Spain. It was quite
logical, therefore, that she was almost equally neutral towards
the Ruthven Raiders, strongly pro-English though they were,
and declined to subsidize them on the scale they craved. Not
only so, but she continued to toy with the idea of an 'Association' of Mary with James.

In pursuing a policy of comparative neutrality towards the
Scottish factions, Elizabeth was refusing to be stampeded by her
ultra-Protestant and Puritan advisers, who constantly advocated
an anti-popish crusade which made no appeal to their Queen's
frigid realism. The force of ultra-Protestant sentiment, which
had an important bearing on Mary's fortunes, was intensified by
the close relations between Elizabeth's Puritan politicians, Walsingham and William Davison, and the Scottish Presbyterians.
The latter had raged against Lennox, whom they persisted in
regarding as the spearhead of a movement to restore Mary and
Catholicism, and they did their best, with considerable success,
to inject their propaganda into the heads of their English associates. There is no doubt of the existence from 1581 or so of
an Anglo-Scottish group, comprising Scottish Presbyterian
ministers and English Puritan politicians, who were determined
to resist all concessions to Mary and to bring about her closer
confinement, if not her execution, and who were far from
scrupulous about the methods to be used to achieve its ends.
One of the most cynical and illuminating remarks of the whole
period was made in this context: 'Bothwell's Casket served for
good uses: there want not Caskets yet.'

When James escaped from the Ruthven Raiders in June 1583,
he inevitably had to rely for a time on a more conservative
element which was favourable to Mary. Not only was there more
talk of an 'Association', but he even wrote to the Pope early in
1584. It was only to be expected that, at Mary's instance, plans
for the Enterprise were revived, though the proposal was now
for a landing in England rather than in Scotland. However, as
James began to feel increasingly secure at home, he had less

need to seek foreign support, and a change in the European situation soon diminished his enthusiasm for continental entanglements. After June 1584, when the Protestant Henry of Navarre became heir to the French throne, the Guises were fully occupied in organizing opposition to the acceptance of a heretical king. The Spaniards, who had never been enthusiastic for a restoration of Mary through French agency, now took up the Enterprise more wholeheartedly. It was evident that Philip was unlikely to conquer England merely in order to hand it over to James, and the latter therefore became more ready to come down firmly on the English and Protestant side. This meant abandoning the cause of his mother, and early in 1585 he categorically repudiated any intention of approving of the 'Association'. In May 1585 a league between Scotland and England was formulated, and it became a binding treaty in July 1586. Mary's claims were quietly ignored.

Mary herself had continued to negotiate energetically with Spain, though Philip and his advisers were beginning to have doubts about conquering England even for her, since her heir was a heretic. She ultimately disinherited her son and made over her rights to Philip, but apparently not until May 1586. Meanwhile the idea had taken shape, in the minds of the most zealous English Roman Catholics as well as in those of the Spaniards, that Philip should ignore James and Mary alike but conquer England and then claim a right to its throne in virtue of his own descent from Edward III. But the Spanish negotiations were highly detrimental to Mary's position. In November 1583 Francis Throckmorton, who had acted as her agent in her intrigues with Spain, was arrested, and under torture revealed that Mary had encouraged the Spaniards in their proposed 'Enterprise'. Various English noblemen and gentlemen who had been involved either fled when they heard of Throckmorton's arrest or were imprisoned. In January 1584 Mendoza, the Spanish ambassador, was dismissed from the English court. In October 1584 the Jesuit Crichton was captured, with papers which revealed more details of the Enterprise. Early in 1585 there was Dr Parry's plot to assassinate Elizabeth, and although Mary expressed quite sincere horror when she heard of it, the fact was that Parry had been in communication with one of her agents.

Those events, combined with the assassination of William the Silent, the Protestant leader in the Netherlands, in June 1584, led to an outburst of feeling in England against Mary, and the Puritan politicians were at this very time receiving additional stimulus from a number of Scottish Presbyterian nobles and ministers who had gone into exile rather than submit to the conservative – and, as they alleged, Marian and pro-Catholic – régime in Scotland. Pressure was so intense that it was beyond Elizabeth's power completely to curb the manifestations of popular sentiment. In October the English council drew up a Bond of Association, which pledged its signatories to contest the succession of any person in whose interest an attempt should be made on Elizabeth's life and to kill that person by any means in their power. The bond was widely signed. In November parliament proposed to authorize it by statute and all Elizabeth could do was to secure the insertion of a modification to the effect that, should Mary become liable to death in terms of the bond, she must first be proved to have been an accomplice to the plot and must be formally tried before being put to death.

In September 1584 Shrewsbury had been superseded as Mary's keeper by Sir Ralph Sadler, who was as considerate as Shrewsbury had been, but in January 1585 she was moved again from Sheffield to Tutbury, with a new gaoler, the unbending Puritan Sir Amias Paulet, who was as impregnable to Mary's charms as John Knox had been. The relations of Mary and Paulet were something like those of Napoleon with Sir Hudson Lowe – a policy of irritating pinpricks on one side, a succession of grievances and complaints on the other. The Paulet régime stopped Mary's secret post, and for a year she was without correspondence. At the end of 1586 Gilbert Gifford, a Roman Catholic sent from the Continent to try to reopen communications with her, was arrested on landing and agreed to play the spy for Walsingham by opening a channel for Mary's correspondence which she would think secret but which would be tapped. On

24 December Mary was transferred to Chartley, where the trap was set. The household received its beer from Burton, and the brewer who supplied it was induced to convey letters to and from Mary in a waterproof packet inserted through the bung-holes of the casks. But every letter that passed was intercepted and copied for Walsingham before being forwarded. The system began to operate in January 1586, and Mary, overjoyed to have means of communication open to her for the first time for a year, launched into a voluminous correspondence.

A few months later, without initial reference to Mary, a band of English Roman Catholics, headed by Anthony Babington, formed a plot for the assassination of Elizabeth as the essential preliminary to any successful invasion from abroad. When Babington disclosed the plot to Mary in July, she – quite possibly instigated by a double-dealing agent – replied with a letter which eagerly welcomed it. She was full of plans for a rescue. The first possibility, she wrote, was that

one day appointed for my walking abroad on horseback, in the moors between this and Stafford, where ordinarily you know that very few people do pass, fifty or three score men horsed and armed come to take me away there, as they may easily do, my keeper having ordinarily with him but eighteen or twenty horsemen, with their dags [heavy pistols]. The second mean is, to come at midnight, or soon after, to set fire to the barns and stables, which, you know, are near to the house; and while my guardian's servants run forth to quench the fire, your company having every one a mark whereby they might know one another under night, might surprise the house, where, I hope, with the few servants that I have about me, I were able to give you correspondence. And the third – some that bring carts thither ordinarily come early in the morning; their carts might be so prepared, and with such cart leaders, that being just in the midst of the gate, the cart might fall down or overwhelm, and you might come suddenly with some followers, and make yourselves masters of the house, and carry me away.

It is true that Mary was an experienced plotter, who had had ample time to devise such ingenious schemes, but it says much

for her irrepressible optimism that, after so many years of captivity, racked with pain and sometimes hardly able to walk, she
was able to write in such terms.

Unfortunately for the captive, a good deal more was involved
than innocent optimism. After she had thus written to Babington, Walsingham pounced, and Mary's papers were seized.
Babington and his fellow conspirators were arrested and, after
they had made confessions incriminating Mary, were executed
in September. Mary's secretaries, taken to London, made further
admissions. The council wanted to have her sent to the Tower,
but Elizabeth decided on Fotheringhay, where Mary arrived on
25 September and where, in October, her second trial began.
She was brought before thirty-six peers, privy councillors, and
judges, on charges of having compassed or imagined acts tending to the hurt of the Queen. Mary's protest that she was no
subject of Elizabeth was set aside, but she defended herself with
dignity, courage, and skill. She admitted that she had attempted
to gain her freedom with the aid of foreign powers, but denied
having sought the Queen's life or even of having corresponded
with Babington. Her original letters could not, of course, be produced as evidence, for after being copied they had been forwarded, but Babington himself, as well as Mary's secretaries,
admitted the accuracy of the copies. Even if the evidence of the
copies was not admitted, and even if the evidence by word of
mouth had been obtained by threats or by hopes of favour,
Mary's own admissions in effect went far enough to make her
guilty of the charge brought against her, for no one could have
believed that Elizabeth would not die in the event of a successful foreign invasion. She was judged guilty, and a few days later
parliament petitioned for her immediate execution.

Elizabeth then entered the final phase of her persistent irresolution towards Mary. She asked parliament if some other way
could be found, short of the death sentence, but the unanimous
answer of both Houses was in the negative. Even after the death-
warrant was signed, on 1 February 1587, Elizabeth tried to
persuade Paulet, as a signatory to the Bond of Association, to
take it upon himself to dispatch his prisoner, but he was too

scrupulous to agree. Even then Elizabeth hesitated, but her secretary, William Davison, took the warrant to the privy council, who on their own responsibility sent it off. The Queen made Davison a scapegoat, and he suffered a term of imprisonment (though without loss of emoluments). It has usually been thought that Elizabeth was at this point wholly insincere and that Davison was badly treated, but there is another side to the matter. Anyone who has read Davison's earlier correspondence on the subject of Mary and on Anglo-Scottish relations generally will conclude not only that sympathy is wasted on him but also that he himself would think his punishment a light price to pay for his part in encompassing Mary's death. A review of Mary's career, with its record of political acumen, tolerance, expediency, and opportunism, makes it impossible to regard her as a martyr for a cause which in fact she adopted wholeheartedly only when all else had failed. At the same time, insufficient attention has been given to the possibility that at the end she *was* a victim – a victim not of Elizabeth, or even of English statesmen and members of parliament, but of a group of fanatics on both sides of the Border, who had pursued her with unscrupulous venom.

Mary was beheaded on 8 February. This woman, who had so often broken down at moments of crisis and who had collapsed when she had to witness the execution of Sir John Gordon in 1562, faced her own end with calm, courage, and dignity.

8   The Continuing Debate

Mary is the one figure in Scottish history who is familiar to people outside Scotland, for the literature about her has made her known to men and women of all nations. Everyone, in every country, or almost every country, has heard of 'Maria Stuart' or whatever they call her in their own tongue. But to see her romantic image as the chief reason for the flood of books about her is an over-simplification. Mary spent nearly nineteen years of her life in England – far longer than she spent in Scotland – and her presence there was a fact of prime importance to the English situation. Therefore, any historian of Tudor England is bound to give a good deal of attention to her. Mary's significance in English history has extended the demand for information about her, and her story cannot be regarded as merely, or even primarily, a part of Scottish history. At the same time, the division of her adult life between her personal rule in Scotland and her captivity in England possibly explains why no wholly satisfactory biography has yet been written. Scottish historians are apt to know little and care less about Mary's life after her flight to England, and from that point tend to carry on the story perfunctorily if they carry it on at all. English historians, equally, are apt to flounder among the unfamiliar institutions and terminology of sixteenth-century Scotland, and their works are marred by ill-considered and uninformed judgments as well as by plain errors. We still await an historian who is equally at home on both sides of the Border and can maintain his interest, as well as his expert knowledge, throughout the whole of Mary's life.

It cannot be said that the explanation of the great output of books on Mary is to be found solely in her personal charm.

Still we look intently [wrote F. W. Maitland] at that wonderful scene, the Scotland of Mary Stewart and John Knox: not merely because it is such glorious tragedy, but also because it is such modern history. The fate of the Protestant Reformation was being decided, and the creed of unborn millions in undiscovered lands was being determined. This we see – all too plainly perhaps – if we read the books that year by year men still are writing of Queen Mary and her surroundings. The patient analysis of those love letters in the casket may yet be perturbed by thoughts about religion. Nor is the religious the only interest. A new nation, a British nation, was in the making.

So there is plenty of material of serious historical concern to justify the interest in Mary. Yet in the books which, for four hundred years now, men have been writing about her, the emphasis has more often been on the tragedy than on the history, for much of the attraction – as well, indeed, as serious historical problems – arise from Mary's fascination, her enigmatic character, the unresolved mysteries which surround her, and the picturesque incidents with which her life was studded.

In her own day, the one man in Scotland whom the Queen could not beguile was John Knox, who was one of the earliest writers on Mary, for he composed part of his *History of the Reformation of Religion within the realm of Scotland* while she was at Holyrood. The inflated importance usually assigned to Knox in any account of the period arises from the fact that he happened to write a book which constitutes his memoirs and is excellent literature, memorable and admirably quotable. But, while Knox had many virtues, humility was not one of them, and his *History* gave a full account of the life and acts of a man about whom other contemporary sources have little or nothing to say. We must constantly remember that the oft-described interviews between Knox and the Queen rest solely on his evidence and that Mary did not leave on record what she thought about it all or what she thought of him. After his first encounter with her, he observed that 'If there be not in her a proud mind, a crafty wit, and an indurate heart against God and His truth, my judgment faileth me.' At another interview, he related, he so upset her that she wept, and his comment was, 'then tears might have been seen, in greater abundance than the matter required'. Knox was clearly determined to be quite unmoved, and one suspects that he was secretly on the defensive, for other episodes in his career show that he was by no means unsusceptible to female charms. At any rate, his attitude was so harsh and unbending that some contemporaries thought it somewhat forced: one of them said that he spoke of Mary as if he were of God's privy council and knew her destiny.

But if Knox was an exception, there is no doubt that Mary captivated others. One may repeat, as a striking illustration, the impression she made on Sir Francis Knollys, an austere Puritan who was not predisposed either by temperament or by principle to favour her. As we saw, Knollys was struck right away by her 'eloquent tongue and discreet head, stout courage, and liberal heart', and at one point he burst out to Cecil: 'What is to be done with such a lady and princess, or whether such a puissant lady be to be nourished in one's bosom, or whether it be good to halt and dissemble with such a lady, I refer to your judgment.'

Perhaps the views of Knox and Knollys, in their contrast, are sufficient to show that even in her own day, as ever since, Mary was the subject of debate. Certainly already in her own lifetime there emerged two irreconcilable images – a sinister and adulterous murderess constantly plotting with every Machiavellian trick to destroy Protestantism in Scotland and England; and, on the other side, a beautiful woman, a devoted wife and mother, and in the end an innocent martyr.

Leaving Knox aside – and he may be left aside, as his work was not published until long after his death – Mary's first great detractor was George Buchanan, and there can be no doubt that Buchanan's writings about Mary had a permanent influence. Buchanan's own record was a curious one. For years he followed convention and wrote verses in praise of Mary – an epithalamium or marriage ode at the time of her marriage to the Dauphin, whom he congratulated on finding a bride rivalling Helen of

Troy in her beauty, and a number of poems in which he lauded her virtue as well as her beauty after she came back to Scotland in 1561. He even dedicated to her his translation of the Psalms. Buchanan, it should be remembered, was a cultivated man who had spent many years on the Continent, he was a considerable scholar and an outstanding Latinist. Like Knox, he met Mary, but in different circumstances, for he was welcome at court, and we are told that of an evening, after supper, Mary sometimes read Livy with him.

But Buchanan changed his tune. As a native of the Lennox, he was in the traditional Scottish manner a client of the Earls of Lennox, the family to which Darnley belonged. Therefore, after Darnley was murdered and Mary blamed for the crime, Buchanan turned fiercely on her as an unfaithful wife and as the murderer of the heir of Lennox. He did not believe in half-measures, for his attacks on Mary are tendentious beyond belief. There was undoubtedly a case to be made against Mary, based on facts, but Buchanan seems at times utterly careless of facts and instead of sticking to them he almost seems to go out of his way to falsify and be inaccurate. He told his tale, with variations, several times over: in his *Detectio Mariae Reginae*, prepared probably in 1568 and translated in 1571 as *Ane Detectioun of the doinges of Marie, Quene of Scottis*; in the Book of Articles which was produced as the indictment of Mary when the charges against her were examined at York and Westminster in 1568; and finally in his *History of Scotland*, published in 1582. The analysis of the Book of Articles in Donaldson's *First Trial of Mary, Queen of Scots* (1969) shows just how wrong Buchanan can sometimes be and how he contradicts established facts which must have been perfectly well known to himself and to his contemporaries. The relevant chapters of the *History* were similarly examined by Dr Gatherer in *The Tyrannous Reign of Mary Stewart* (1958). When Buchanan was asked whether he thought it tactful, during the reign of Mary's son, to blacken her character as he was doing, he retorted, 'Tell me if I have told the truth.' But his concept of truth was such a presentation of events as fitted with his own theories and preconceptions. A recent commentator has remarked, 'The plain fact, surely, is that Buchanan was not an historian, was incapable of taking the historian's view of human development, and was indifferent to the rules of historical evidence.'

It has to be remembered that Buchanan's *History*, which won a renown reflecting the fame of the author as one of Scotland's outstanding literary men, long held the field as the standard comprehensive history of Scotland. In some respects it was not superseded until the nineteenth century. This means that Buchanan's version of events had a long innings, and although it was often challenged it tended to be the book which most people read and believed. It therefore created and maintained what can be called the normal or conventional point of view, and a lot of it is still repeated even now as, in effect, the authorized version.

The first to challenge Buchanan was John Lesley, Bishop of Ross, who wrote his *Defence of the Honour of the Right High, Mighty and Noble Princess Mary, Queen of Scotland and Dowager of France*, and published it anonymously in 1569. Lesley was concerned not only to defend Mary against Buchanan's calumnies, but also to defend the right of women to rule and the right of Mary to succeed Elizabeth. Like Buchanan, he subsequently incorporated his findings in a *History of Scotland*, published in Latin in 1578, four years before Buchanan's. But, although some of Lesley's work was often republished and was quite well known, especially among continental Roman Catholics, it was on the whole less influential than Buchanan's. To Protestants, Lesley was suspect as a Roman Catholic, whom they deemed incapable of telling the truth about Mary. This was unfair, for Lesley did not have a very strong religious bias and he is never as flagrantly and deliberately mendacious as Buchanan is. On the other hand, when he can be checked he can often be shown to be inaccurate in detail, though probably as a result of carelessness and some self-deception rather than of conscious distortion. All in all, he did not deserve to be very influential.

As the years went on, in the later sixteenth century, the field in which Buchanan and Lesley had originally clashed, namely the question whether Mary was guilty of adultery and murder, tended to recede into the background. It was Mary's religious position that became the prominent issue, and her defenders became more and more concerned to present her as a Roman Catholic martyr. This trend can be detected long before her execution, during the years when she might perhaps have been reckoned a 'confessor' rather than a 'martyr'. One very influential writer in setting a fashion was the Englishman Nicholas Sanders, who as early as 1571, in *De visibili monarchia Ecclesiae*, enrolled Mary among the list of sufferers for the Roman Catholic faith in England. Sanders, who expanded his views in later writing, was not content with whitewashing Mary, but also vilified Elizabeth and her mother, Anne Boleyn, to the extent of showing a disregard for the truth and a fondness for invention which put him in the same class as Buchanan. Sanders anticipated the propaganda of the Counter-Reformation, which began to be active in England in the 1580s. Mary's situation as a captive, and in Roman Catholic and continental eyes an undeserving captive, could be used to stimulate English Roman Catholics and continental powers to action against Elizabeth on her behalf. Mary was fitted into this context not only in the posthumous work by Sanders, *The Rise and growth of the Anglican schism*, published at Rheims in 1585, but also in Cardinal William Allen's *Defence of the English Catholics*, published at Ingoldstadt in 1584.

Sanders, like Buchanan on the other side, had shown how invention could come in, and there was more invention when Mary was finally beheaded, for accounts of her execution were good propaganda and could only too easily be embroidered to make the tale even more pitiable than it really was. There were accounts produced in French, Italian, German, and Dutch, some of them making out not only that Mary had been executed because she was a Catholic, but also that she had been deposed on account of her religion and that Elizabeth had inveigled her into England on promise of assistance before unjustly holding her a prisoner. One of the tales related that Mary arrived in England in 1568 only because her ship had been blown off course when she had been making for France – a statement which many people, only twenty years after the event, must have known to be a misrepresentation. There were also verses in Latin and French, largely the work of Adam Blackwood, a Scot who had settled in France as a student and teacher of law and philosophy. Blackwood's verses denounced Elizabeth as a Jezebel and called for action against her, but, like the other works just mentioned, they resorted to invention, for Elizabeth was accused of having tried in person to poison Mary and it was alleged that the English Queen had several illegitimate children. But Blackwood was a scholar, who produced in 1581 his *Apologia pro regibus*, which defended Mary's sovereignty and condemned her deposition by heretics, and immediately after Mary's execution he produced his *Martyre de la royne d'Escosse*, which is a medley of serious thought and scurrility. The scurrility takes the shape of wild accusations against Elizabeth for immorality, and wilder accusations against her mother. The serious element included an allegation that the Babington Plot, which led directly to Mary's execution, was really a fabrication by the English government, and here Blackwood anticipated some recent writers. His works were extremely influential on the Roman Catholic side, and many later books borrowed from him.

There are then, in Buchanan and Sanders and Blackwood, plenty of examples of fancies and fictions contained in works which were professedly factual. But there were other writings which made no such profession. Maitland, after all, said that Mary's reign was not only 'modern history' but also 'glorious tragedy'. And it was not long before the dramatists saw its potential. The historical novel had not yet been invented, and historical fiction found its expression in pseudo-historical dramas whose authors were the forerunners not only of the historical novelists but also of the writers of film and television scripts. An early example was *Maria Stuarta Tragoedia*, a school play written by a French Jesuit in 1589. This, in presenting the last twenty-four hours of Mary's life, takes enormous liberties with the facts. There are quite imaginary scenes of discussions among English councillors, appeals by foreign ambassadors who suc-

ceeded in persuading Elizabeth to agree to spare Mary, and then
the contrary and successful efforts of the villainous English to
have that decision reversed. At the end an angel appears to
Mary, assuring her of an eternal reward as a blessed martyr, and
after her death King James arrives on the scene to have an
interview with her ghost.

There was a certain appropriateness in the fantasy of introducing James in this way, because presently his attitude was to
have some influence on the trend of the writings about his
mother. James, it need hardly be said, had no affection for a
mother from whom he had been separated when he was a year
old, and he probably had not grieved at her execution. But at
the same time it was inconsistent with his dignity to have his
mother's honour called in question, and he was ready to rise to
her defence on paper, though he had done so little for her in
deeds. As early as 1596, when Edmund Spenser's Faerie Queene
accused Mary of murder and adultery, an offended James protested to the English ambassador. After 1603, when he became
King of England, his opinion carried more weight, and writers
on Mary learned that they had to exercise some discretion if
they were not to offend the King of Great Britain. When Jacques
de Thou, in the second volume of his History of his own Time
(1607), reproduced Buchanan's fictions, James, who had already
attempted to suppress Buchanan's History, commissioned the
English historian William Camden to draw up a list of the false-
hoods which de Thou had repeated. Therefore, when Camden
came to write his own Annals (1615), he was ready to adopt
a critical attitude to Buchanan and to rely rather on Lesley,
exonerating Mary from immorality and at the same time putting the blame for her downfall not on her religion but on the
political ambitions of Moray, Morton, and their fellows. James
gave further evidence of his ostensible respect for his mother's
memory when, in 1612, he had her body removed from Peterborough Cathedral to Westminster Abbey.

During the rest of the seventeenth century there may not
have been exactly an armistice in the controversy, but there
was certainly a lull, and this serves to mark off contemporary

and near-contemporary works from the products of a period
when Mary had become a more remote historical figure. The
sixteenth-century writers had relied very largely on what they
had themselves heard, and what they were writing about was,
in a sense, current affairs rather than history. But when we pass
over the seventeeth century and come to the eighteenth we
encounter writers who had to rely not on their own recollections
or first-hand knowledge, or even on hearsay, but on documentary evidence. The habit of collecting and printing documents
was not indeed a novelty of the eighteenth century, for the
fashion had been well established earlier. John Knox had been
a conspicuous example of a writer who reproduced a great
many original documents, and in the generation after him the
Presbyterian historian David Calderwood wrote a *History of
the Church of Scotland* which consists very largely of original
documents. On the Presbyterian side the tradition was continued
in the early eighteenth century by Robert Wodrow, whose two
massive folios on *The Sufferings of the Church of Scotland* contain hundreds of documents and extracts from the public records
of Scotland. Although they relate not to the sixteenth century
but to the period between the Restoration and the Revolution,
they set an example which was to be followed by writers on the
earlier period.

When the Marian controversy was resumed in the eighteenth
century it was in the context of the reproduction of original
documents. Some of the collecting and publishing of source
material was quite disinterested and represented pure scholarship, in the sense that it was not designed to support a case or
further a particular argument. There were the volumes of state
papers printed by Patrick Forbes, William Murdin, and Samuel
Haynes between 1740 and 1759, largely from the Cecil Collection at Hatfield. In Scotland there were Walter Ruddiman's
two volumes of *Letters of the Scottish Kings* (1722–4), containing
correspondence of James IV, James V, and Mary. None of these
were designed primarily as contributions to Marian literature.
But there were other collections of documents selected because
they related specifically to Mary. Samuel Jebb, in *De Vita et*

rebus gestis Mariae (2 vols., 1725), brought together pamphlets and other material. James Anderson edited four volumes of *Collections relating to Mary, Queen of Scots* (1727–8). Walter Goodall, another of the documentary scholars of the period, produced two volumes with the title *An examination of the letters alleged to have been written by Mary, Queen of Scots, to the Earl of Bothwell* (1754). His intention was to prove that the Casket Letters were forgeries, on the argument that the existing French copies had been translated from Scots, which Mary would not have used; but one of his volumes is a solid collection of documents, largely from the English State Papers, and this has been so valuable that it has been extensively used by all later writers on Mary, whether or not they have accepted Goodall's arguments against the genuineness of the Casket Letters. The counter-argument to Goodall was of course that the Scots versions had themselves been first translated from French.

Midway between mere collections of documents and books designed to present a narrative is Robert Keith's *History of the Affairs of Church and State in Scotland in the Reigns of Mary and James VI*; the first volume (the only one published), dealing with the reign of Mary, appeared in 1734. Keith prints a very large number of documents, but a lot of them are strung together in the course of a narrative. Keith was not very tendentious, but rather the faithful historian and record scholar presenting the source material without commenting much upon it. Like Goodall, he has been of immense value to everyone who has followed him.

Then we come to the writers who were concerned less with the presentation of documents than with writing what they conceived to be history and telling a story. Outstanding among them was William Robertson, a leading divine of the Church of Scotland and principal of Edinburgh University, who produced his *History of Scotland in the Reigns of Mary and James VI* in 1759. Robertson, unlike Keith, was not an enthusiastic record scholar: 'Much still remained in darkness, unobserved and unpublished. It was my duty to search for these, and I found this unpleasant task attended with considerable utility.' Far too much of a gentleman to enjoy delving in the dust and grime of ancient records, Robertson leaned heavily on Keith, without whom he could never have written such a copious account of Mary's reign. Robertson's is almost history of a new kind, for there is more analysis, far more study of cause and effect, far more characterization of personalities, than in earlier books. But, despite reliance on Keith, and despite the work of Goodall, Robertson in his findings was content in the main to follow the familiar narratives of Buchanan and other anti-Marian writers. He wrote, of course, as a Whig and a Presbyterian and could not be predisposed to favour Mary. Robertson's contemporary, David Hume, also wrote a *History* of the period, published in the same year as Robertson's, though it is a history of England, not of Scotland. Hume, as a Tory and half a Jacobite, was more sympathetically disposed than Robertson to the Stewarts, but he does not present a substantially more favourable picture of Mary.

Hard on the heels of Robertson and Hume came William Tytler's *Inquiry Historical and Critical into the evidence against Mary, Queen of Scots, and an Examination of the Histories of Dr Robertson and Mr Hume with respect to that evidence.* Tytler reverted to Goodall's position and absolved Mary from guilt. John Whitaker, in *Mary, Queen of Scots, vindicated* (1787), and Thomas Crawford, in *The History of Mary, Queen of Scots* (1793), both took the same line and presented Mary as above reproach. Nearly half a century elapsed after Tytler's work before there was a major counter-blast from the other side, but in 1804 Malcolm Laing produced two volumes of a *Preliminary Dissertation on the participation of Mary, Queen of Scots, in the murder of Darnley*, in which he set aside Goodall, Tytler, Whitaker, and Crawford and adjudged Mary guilty.

So the two conflicting points of view had been well ventilated with substantial scholarship, in the second half of the eighteenth century and the beginning of the nineteenth. There were no signs that one or the other was going to prevail, but on the whole the critics of Mary were thought to have the better case. Sir Walter Scott, just a few years after Laing's work, refused to write a biography of Mary, 'because', as he put it, 'his opinion was contrary to his feeling'. In other words, he was not willing to face the fact that Mary really had been guilty. However, in his *Tales of a Grandfather* he goes so far as to admit that 'she may have been criminal'.

The nineteenth century added even more than the eighteenth to the amount of source material that was available in print. The Scottish publishing clubs, especially the Maitland and Bannatyne, naturally produced a certain amount of new material, like the *Affaires du Comte de Bothwell* (Bothwell's own account of his career), the *Inventories of Queen Mary*, giving details of her jewels and other possessions, the *Memoirs of Lord Herries*, one of Mary's supporters, and the *Diurnal of Occurrents*, a valuable diary of the period; and they also reprinted older publications like Sir James Melville's *Memoirs* and the *Histories* of Lesley and Knox. From France, too, there came important contributions, in Prince Labanoff's edition of Mary's *Letters*, in seven volumes (1844), and several volumes of papers selected by Alexandre Teulet from the French archives. As the century went on, there was a perfect flood of official publications in which English and Scottish records were printed. Especially important were the *Calendars of State Papers* – English diplomatic correspondence with Spain, Venice, the Papal Court, and, not least, Scotland. Then there were, from Scottish records, the *Treasurer's Accounts*, the *Register of the Great Seal*, the *Register of the Privy Council*, and so on. Besides these editions of material in official custody, the Historical MSS Commission, first appointed in 1870, printed many papers from private collections in England and Scotland. An outstanding discovery resulting from the examination of private papers was that of the dispensation for the marriage of Bothwell to Lady Jane Gordon; the lady later married the Earl of Sutherland and carefully preserved the dispensation, which was found among the Sutherland archives. At the end of the century the Scottish History Society began to make a further contribution to the printed sources, especially with J. H. Pollen's volumes on the relations of Mary with Roman Catholic powers.

Clearly, then, there was a vast amount of fresh printed material at the disposal of the historians who turned their attention to Mary in the late nineteenth century and the beginning of the twentieth. Between 1870 and 1874 John Hosack produced *Mary, Queen of Scots, and Her Accusers*, an able defence of Mary which scored some good points and which made hay – which it was not difficult to do – of a lot of the old tales which had come down from Buchanan. T. F. Henderson gave special attention to the *Casket Letters* (1889), and in a two-volume *Life of Mary* which he brought out in 1905 – the best biography to appear until Lady Antonia Fraser's in 1969 – he argued that the letters were genuine. Henderson's antagonist was Andrew Lang, a voluminous and spirited writer on innumerable topics. Lang's sympathies were invariably on the royalist and conservative side, and he was not likely to appear in any other part than as a defender of Mary. However, although in his original edition of *The Mystery of Mary Stewart*, published in 1901, Lang defended Mary and contended that the Casket Letters were forgeries, he later modified his opinions, and when he prepared the last edition of his book in 1912 he announced that he was converted to Henderson's view that the Casket Letters were genuine.

Perhaps the most valuable contribution to Marian scholarship in that period was made by David Hay Fleming. Fleming, like Lang, had his prejudices, but they were diametrically opposed to Lang's, for Fleming was an ultra-Presbyterian. While Lang was more a journalist than a scholar, Fleming was a scholar through and through, and everything he put down could be fully supported by documentary evidence. He hit on the useful idea, for which every subsequent historian of Mary must bless him, of writing in 1897 *The Life of Queen Mary from her birth to her flight into England*, a curious work, in which the text is a mere summary and the bulk of the book consists of supporting notes which are references to and quotations from the original sources. It might almost have been thought of as the book to end all books on the subject, but it is less a book for the general reader than a quarry for scholars which takes its place with Keith and Goodall among the indispensable equipment of the student of the period. It might have been used even more if it had an index.

Between the wars, the outstanding novelty came in the work of Major-General R. H. Mahon, especially in *The Tragedy of Kirk o' Field* (1930). Mahon advanced the theory that the Kirk o' Field plot was not a plot by Mary against Darnley but a plot by Darnley against Mary. The Queen was the intended victim, and Darnley was plotting to replace her and rule with the support of the Roman Catholic powers. Mahon's work makes some very ingenious and important points, not least about the precise *locus* of the crime, and he offers suggestions that no one can dismiss. Yet his thesis as a whole has not won acceptance. Mahon was not a trained historian, he was somewhat slapdash in presenting his evidence and his authorities, and this means that some of his findings have carried less weight than they might otherwise have done. Besides, his thesis, despite its many attractions, does not explain everything. To the same generation and the same school belongs Robert Gore-Browne, who wrote his *Lord Bothwell* in 1937. Gore-Browne followed the general thesis of Mahon, but with some refinements, for, whereas Mahon had been content with two plots and two bands of murderers, Gore-Browne went further and postulated three – Darnley's supporters, who placed the gunpowder in the vaults below Kirk o' Field with the intention of blowing up Mary; Bothwell, who just happened to be strolling past, noticed the powder, and put a match to it; and the followers of Morton, who, by a curious coincidence, happened to be in the garden when Darnley fled from the house, and coolly strangled him. Not many would accept all this. Yet Gore-Browne's spirited defence of his hero commands respect, and since he wrote no one should have been content with the shallow view of Bothwell as a dastardly villain.

One of the most useful books to appear since the Second World War is Dr Armstrong Davidson's study of the *Casket Letters* (1965), which reprints the text of the letters in full. Davidson attempts to disentangle the various parts of the letters and trace how the existing text was constructed out of partly genuine, partly manipulated, and partly forged material. He believes in Mary's innocence and takes Mahon's view that the main plot in 1567 was one against Mary, inspired by Darnley. Whether or not the reader accepts Dr Davidson's conclusions, this is a very useful book. Meantime the traditional view – the classical view of Buchanan – was not abandoned, but was resurrected by George Malcolm Thomson in *The Crime of Mary Stewart* (1967).

The opening shot in a campaign to exonerate Roman Catholics from charges of plotting to murder English sovereigns was fired as far back as 1897, when J. Gerard put forward the theory that the Gunpowder Plot was not a plot by Roman Catholics at all, but a fabrication by the government to bring discredit on the papists. More recently *The Marvellous Chance* by Francis Edwards (1968) and *An Elizabethan Problem* by Leo Hicks (1964) seek to dispose of the Ridolfi Plot and the Babington Plot in the same way. Both the authors were Jesuits, and they take the view that these plots were machinations of the English government, designed ultimately to bring Mary to the scaffold.

Amid such a cloud – or fog – of witnesses it is hardly surprising that two of the most useful recent works have been not books about Mary but books about the books about Mary. James E. Phillips, in *Images of a Queen* (1964), traces the growth of the opposing schools of thought down to the early seventeenth century. Ian B. Cowan, in *The Enigma of Mary Stuart* (1971), surveys the whole debate, with appropriate extracts from a wide range of writings.

Select Bibliography

The discussion in the last chapter of the main works on Mary obviates the need for an extended bibliography, but it may be useful to draw attention to the books which can most profitably be read, especially those which are at present in print. Many of those books themselves contain bibliographies, and Conyers Read, *Bibliography of British History, Tudor Period* (2nd edn, Oxford University Press, 1959), will help the student to find his way about the original sources and track down some of the older secondary books which can still be usefully referred to.

Among the easily accessible sources which any reader will find rewarding, John Knox's *History of the Reformation* (ed. W. Croft Dickinson, 2 vols., Nelson, 1949), a narrative of events by one of the principal actors, is outstanding as literature as well as history. Equally readable are the *Memoirs of Sir James Melville of Halhill*, to be found in full in the Bannatyne Club edition (Edinburgh, 1827) and in abridged form in the Folio Society edition (London, 1969). A handy collection of extracts from the main source material is W. Croft Dickinson, Gordon Donaldson, and Isabel A. Milne, *A Source Book of Scottish History*, vol. ii (2nd edn, Nelson, 1958). W. A. Gatherer's *Tyrannous Reign of Mary Stewart* (Edinburgh University Press, 1958), an edition of the relevant portions of George Buchanan's *History*, is instructive as to the extent to which a near-contemporary could distort and invent evidence.

The Scottish background is presented in G. Donaldson, *Scotland: James V to James VII* (Oliver & Boyd, 1965), and *The Scottish Reformation* (Cambridge University Press, 1960). The English background is to be found in J. B. Black, *The Reign of Elizabeth*

(2nd edn, Oxford University Press, 1955), and J. E. Neale, *Queen Elizabeth I* (Cape, 1934). The circumstances surrounding Mary's captivity in England and the plots of her later years are fully described in Conyers Read, *Mr Secretary Walsingham and the policy of Queen Elizabeth* (3 vols., Oxford University Press, 1925), and J. E. Neale, *Elizabeth I and her Parliament* (2 vols., Cape, 1953, 1957).

The best full-length study in print is Antonia Fraser, *Mary, Queen of Scots* (Weidenfeld & Nicholson, 1969), and the best of the older biographies is T. F. Henderson, *Mary, Queen of Scots* (2 vols., Hutchinson, 1905). Hay Fleming's *Mary, Queen of Scots* (Hodder & Stoughton, 1897), described in chapter 8, is the indispensable work of reference as well as a streamlined narrative of Mary's life to 1568.

It is perhaps unprofitable for others than specialists to go to the older writings on the great debate about Mary's guilt. J. Hosack, *Mary, Queen of Scots, and her Accusers* (2 vols., Blackwood, 1874), remains the ablest defence. The question of guilt of course centres largely on the Kirk o' Field mystery and the Casket Letters, and the reader will do well to look at some earlier works, like T. F. Henderson's *Casket Letters* (2nd edn, Black, 1890) and Andrew Lang's *Mystery of Mary Stewart* (3rd edn, Longmans, 1912), as well as more recent works like R. H. Mahon, *The Tragedy of Kirk o' Field* (Cambridge University Press, 1930), and M. H. Armstrong Davidson, *The Casket Letters* (Vision Press, 1965).

Other important biographies are by Maurice Lee, *James Stewart, Earl of Moray* (Columbia University Press, 1953), Eustace Percy, *John Knox* (Hodder & Stoughton, 1937), and Robert Gore-Browne, *Lord Bothwell* (Collins, 1937).

James E. Phillips, *Images of a Queen* (University of California Press, 1964), is concerned with the writings of Mary's contemporaries and near-contemporaries and their conflicting points of view. Ian B. Cowan, *The Enigma of Mary Stuart* (Gollancz, 1971), is valuable as a review of the whole debate, not only in writings of Mary's own day but as it has been conducted over the centuries.

Index